MARK PATTISON
AND THE IDEA OF A
UNIVERSITY

THE CLARK LECTURES
1965

MARK PATTISON
AND THE IDEA OF A
UNIVERSITY

BY

JOHN SPARROW

Warden of All Souls College, Oxford

CAMBRIDGE
AT THE UNIVERSITY PRESS
1967

Published by the Syndics of the Cambridge University Press
Bentley House, 200 Euston Road, London, N.W. 1
American Branch: 32 East 57th Street, New York, N.Y. 10022

© Cambridge University Press 1967

Library of Congress Catalogue Card Number: 67-12141

Printed in Great Britain
at the University Printing House, Cambridge
(Brooke Crutchley, University Printer)

TO
JOHN BRYSON

CONTENTS

*The frontispiece reproduces a photograph
of Mark Pattison taken in about 1880
and now in the possession of the author.*

PREFACE

The lectures that make up this book were delivered, in a shorter form, in Cambridge in the autumn of 1965. I should like to record here my gratitude to the Master and Fellows of Trinity College for honouring me with the invitation to be Clark Lecturer and for the friendly hospitality with which they welcomed me when the lectures were delivered.

When I was invited by the Syndics of the University Press to submit the lectures for publication, I hesitated; I was conscious (as I still am) of how much they suffer from being the work of an inexperienced lecturer and an untrained historian, and of how far my clumsy and superficial patchwork falls short of doing justice to its subject. In accepting the Syndics' invitation I yielded to feelings that I tried to express in the last lecture (pp. 133-4, 146-9): I am sure that Pattison's personality—which I have done my best, however inadequately, to bring to life in the first two lectures—deserves to be better appreciated and more widely known; and I believe that the sketch of his experience of Oxford reform contained in the third and fourth lectures, superficial though it is, may suggest lessons that should be of profit to the University today.

I must mention two books that provide a detailed background to the historical and personal sides, respectively, of my story: the first (which did not come out, unfortunately, until my work on the lectures was already far advanced) is Mr W. R. Ward's *Victorian Oxford* which contains an exceedingly detailed account of the history and literature of reform in the University in the nineteenth century; the second is Mr V. H. H. Green's *Oxford Common Room*, which paints a lively and authentic picture of Lincoln College, and its Head, during Pattison's Rectorship. Mr Green's book, like mine, is based on a close familiarity with the thousands of pages of the Pattison MSS. in the Bodleian, and those who have read *Oxford Common Room* will recognize in my first and second lectures several passages quoted by him from Pattison's correspondence. I should like to assure such readers, and Mr Green himself, that this is not a case of plagiarism, and that every one (I believe) of these quotations was among a number of passages that I had transcribed from the MSS. before his book was published.

All Souls College, Oxford   JOHN SPARROW
November 1966

PATTISON AND THE NOVELISTS

Mark Pattison is probably thought of today, by those who remember him at all, as the rival of Jowett in the field of University reform; as the author of a remarkable book of *Memoirs*; perhaps, as the hero, or anti-hero, of a famous Oxford intrigue; and as a very learned man. People with specialized interests may be able to go further: scholars will connect his name with Isaac Casaubon, of whom he wrote a classic biography, and readers of George Eliot may be aware of a different association with the same name: was he not Mr Casaubon, the hero, or (again) the anti-hero, of *Middlemarch*?

Even to those who know so much about him, Pattison, I suspect, remains little more than a name; they do not see him as a living man. And that is not surprising. He published little—his study of Casaubon; an excellent short Life of Milton; a tract on University Reform; first-rate editions of Milton's sonnets and of certain of Pope's poems; and a number of articles on literary and historical subjects, the best of which were collected and published in two volumes after his death. His life's work—a History of European learning, built round a biography of Joseph Scaliger—never took shape as a book. And what he did publish was not work of the sort that reveals the character of its author, nor yet of the sort that impels the reader to inquire: 'The man who wrote that, what must he have been like?'

But once you have read Pattison's posthumous *Memoirs*, you want to find out more about him. And when you get to know him, you cannot help wanting to introduce him to others. He was the most perfect English example of an uncommon type—the man whose life was dedicated to his mind; not the consummate scholar, like Bentley, but the living encyclopaedia of organized knowledge. In this he represented his own ideal: 'Learning', he said, 'is a peculiar compound of memory, imagination, scientific habit, accurate observation, all concentrated, through a prolonged period, on the analysis of the remains of literature. The result of this sustained mental endeavour is not a book, but a man.'

Pattison was such a man; but he was more than that: he was an extraordinary human being; he made an unforgettable impression, not always an agreeable one, upon almost every one who met him. Before I try to reproduce that impression, I had better sketch, in the fewest possible words, the framework of his life.

Pattison was born, in a Yorkshire parsonage, in 1813; he went up to Oriel in the year of the Reform Bill; was elected a Fellow of Lincoln in 1839; took Orders, and nearly followed Newman to Rome in 1845; just failed to become the Head of his College in 1851; achieved that position ten years later; and died in 1884. In 1861, the year he became Rector of Lincoln, he married Emilia Francis Strong, a girl twenty-seven years his junior and almost as remarkable a person as he was himself: the marriage was childless; she survived him, and a year after his death became the wife of Sir Charles Dilke. She died in 1904.

Pattison devoted his career to Oxford and to learning. He was not exactly an academic hermit; he enjoyed the open air; even in middle age he could 'bustle an Oxford hack across the country side' after hounds, and to the end of his life he spent months in every year alone with rod and line; in his middle years he made several prolonged visits to Germany, and in later days he became a familiar figure at the Athenaeum, at such gatherings as the Social Science Congress, and in intellectual circles in London. But his real life was lived in his library at Lincoln: 'I am fairly entitled to say', he declared in 1883, a few months before his death, 'that, since the year 1851, I have lived wholly for study.'

When he died, Pattison was, in the smaller and more compactly civilized England of a hundred years ago, a well-known figure. *The Times* devoted the best part of a page to his obituary, and declared that by his death the country had lost 'a master mind'.

Records of the impression that he made on his contemporaries are to be found in many volumes of Victorian correspondence and reminiscence, and the impression was usually a vivid one. Swinburne, to whom Pattison represented all that was least attractive in Oxford, contrasted his own patron Jowett with 'such spiritually and morally typical and unmistakable apes of the Dead Sea as Mark Pattison'.

One who was a pupil, but by no means an admirer, gives a more measured judgement of his personality:

Pattison's temperament [says John Morley], his reading, his recoil from Catholicism, combined with his strong reflective

3   I-2

powers to produce an infinitely curious and salient personality. There was no one in whose company one felt quite so safe against an attack of platitude. There was no one on whom one could so surely count for some stroke of irony or pungent suggestion, or, at the worst, some significant, admonitory, and luminous manifestation of the great *ars tacendi* . . .

His silences were famous; they made undergraduates dread the prospect of an afternoon walk not broken even by the Rector's famous snarl.

The best account of what Pattison looked like in his later years comes from a pupil, T. F. Althaus:

His face was pale with the pale cast of thought, and the deep lines with which it was marked were the result rather of hard thinking than of age. The thin, reddish moustache and beard, and the short, slightly-curling brown hair, showed little or no trace of grey; but the somewhat sunken mouth, with the consequent convergence of nose and chin, helped to give the face an aged appearance. This served, however, to bring into prominence the singular brightness of the grey eye, which, whether 'glittering', as it has been well described, with the light of some fresh thought, or fixed, as it occasionally was, in the compassionless rigidity of a 'stony glare', or mild, almost melting at times, with sympathy, was always deep and searching, and must be regarded as his most striking feature. His voice, in unconstrained conversation, was soft and pleasant; but in official intercourse, or when he was severe, the utterance, accompanying the 'stony glare', would become harsh and nasal; and there were some who, as they expressed it, had only heard the Rector 'snarl'.

Here is a last portrait, drawn by Stephen Gwynne:

In 1883 or 1884 a group of figures entering the Radcliffe Square at Oxford made a lasting mark on my mind. Mark Pattison,

Rector of Lincoln, drawn in a bath-chair by a shambling menial, lay more like a corpse than any living thing I have ever seen. And yet there was a singular vitality behind that parchment covered face: something powerful and repellent. Beside him walked his wife, small, erect, and ultra Parisian: all in black with a black parasol—I did not know then how often Frenchwomen thus enhance the brilliance of a personality: still less did I know how few but Frenchwomen could do it. But there, plain to be seen for the least accustomed eyes, was the gift of style. No less plainly, her presence conveyed detachment from her convoy with an emphasis that absence could never have given. Either of these two figures alone would have arrested even the least observant eye: together, they presented dramatically the spectacle of an amazing marriage to which the world's attention had already been called.

These are vivid presentations. But for a really living picture we must go not to the photographers but to the painters. As Pattison himself observed: 'If truth is stranger than fiction, fiction has its revenge in being truer than fact. It is the privilege of the novelist, as of the artist, to place before us the truth which is in things, but which is concealed by the facts.'

The place in Victorian fiction that one naturally turns to if one is looking for a portrait of Mark Pattison is Mallock's *New Republic*. That brilliant conversation-piece came out in 1876,[1] when Pattison's reputation was at its zenith; to Mallock, who had just taken his degree, the Rector of Lincoln must have been a familiar figure; he included Jowett in his portrait-gallery, and Pater, and Matthew Arnold; Carlyle is there, and Ruskin; there is even a glimpse of Dr Pusey; and one of the minor characters has

[1] In *Belgravia*; it was published as a book in the following year.

been, for no good reason, identified with Mrs Mark Pattison. But Pattison is absent, and (to me at any rate) his absence is a mystery. For a *pastiche* of Pattison in a university setting the world has had to wait half a century for the brilliant parody of his *Memoirs* in Mgr Ronald Knox's *Let Dons Delight.*

Three writers of fiction—among them one of the most admired of English novelists—felt the force of Pattison's personality intensely enough to reproduce it, more or less faithfully, in their books. All three were women; and that is not surprising, for Pattison was interesting to women in a way in which he was not interesting to men.

Of the three novelists who put Pattison, in one way or another, into their books I will take first Rhoda Broughton —'Our dear Rhoda, our gallant and intrepid Rhoda', she was called by Henry James, who thought her 'admirable and wonderful'. She was an acid and indomitable spinster who, as she said herself, began life as Zola and ended it— she did not die until the 1920s—as Charlotte M. Yonge. Her luxuriantly sentimental novels—*Cometh Up As A Flower* and *Not Wisely, But Too Well* were two of the most popular—are readable now only for their vivid but superficial pictures of Victorian social life; but she was thought daring eighty years ago; she was a shrewd observer, she had a sharp tongue, and she was no respecter of persons. She was already a popular novelist and a familiar Oxford figure when, in 1883, she published *Belinda.*

I will not recapitulate the plot of this crude and childish three-volume novel; it is enough to say that a very ordinary girl believes she has been jilted by the young hero, and impulsively marries Mr James Forth, Professor of Etruscan in Oxbridge University. The professor is a mean, pedantic, hypochondriacal egotist, who uses his young wife as an unpaid secretary. We are not told that he was a fraud; but the reader cannot help having his suspicions about a Professor of Etruscan whose *magnum opus* is an edition of the fragments of Menander, and who apparently relies upon St Augustine and Irenaeus as authorities for his text.

Belinda, condemned to a loveless and joyless existence in North Oxford, bitterly regrets her mistake, but is duly restored to the man she loves by the professor's providential death.

The background, and the relation between the principal figures, find their exact counterparts in the Rector of Lincoln and his wife; and there are plenty of particular touches that identify Pattison with Professor Forth: the meanness of the 'old skinflint' is a perpetual theme; he is always out of humour, and his ill-humour 'renders yet more pinched and captious his pinched pedant face', he talks like a book—one of Pattison's books: 'You must be aware', he declares, 'that the whole tendency of my teaching is to show that the pursuit of knowledge is the only one that abundantly rewards the labour bestowed upon it.' He has a 'contempt for undergraduates' and does not often look at them 'because he dislikes them too much'; but he enjoys 'forming the minds' of intelligent young women, and reads Browning to them while they sit round in an admiring circle.

7

The superficial picture is accurate enough; that, no doubt, was how Pattison appeared to most people who met him but did not know him well.[1] And I can quote an episode that proves that Rhoda Broughton was indeed drawing from the life.

Belinda, like *Mansfield Park*, was a 'three-decker' novel, and Rhoda Broughton, like Jane Austen, took advantage of the three-volume form. You will remember the private theatricals so improperly got up by the party at Mansfield Park during the absence of Sir Thomas Bertram and so dramatically interrupted by his unexpected return. 'My father is come; he is in the hall at this moment'—Jane Austen makes these terrible words all the more effective by placing them as the closing words of the first volume of the book.

A similar episode closes the second volume of *Belinda*. Professor Forth, supposed to be presiding over a meeting of 'The Archaeological Society', returns unexpectedly to find Belinda and her sister enjoying themselves with a party of undergraduates; exhausted with an improvised dance, they have betaken themselves to blind man's buff; at the height of their merriment, an 'instantaneous and entire muteness falls upon the so boisterous little assemblage', and Belinda 'tears the bandage from her eyes', to see that 'The door is half open, and through it Professor Forth is looking, with an expression hard to qualify upon his face, at the entertainment got up with such spirit and success in his absence'.

[1] Certainly the caricature, superficial though it was, was recognized in Oxford: see D. S. MacColl in *The Nineteenth Century*, January 1945, pp. 28–33 and *The Oxford Review*, 21 January 1885.

Rhoda Broughton, when she wrote that, may well have been recalling *Mansfield Park*; she was certainly recalling life. The following story was told me by an honorary fellow of Lincoln, who had it from one of the undergraduates who were at the party:

One night, when Pattison had gone out to dinner, Mrs P. and her rather giddy sister had got in a number of undergraduates to an impromptu party. At a moment when they had done up all the men's hair in curl papers, the door opened unexpectedly and the Rector walked in. He punished them effectively by going round the room, and very slowly and ceremoniously shaking hands with all present, while they wished that the floor would swallow them up.

No wonder that when Pattison next called on Miss Broughton in Holywell he asked the parlour-maid to announce him as 'Professor Forth'.

My second portrait comes from a more perceptive writer, George Eliot. The question whether *Middlemarch* contains a portrait of the Rector has exercised readers and critics ever since the book was published. George Eliot's admirers have been unwilling to admit it. 'There never was a more impertinent blunder', said John Morley, 'than when people professed to identify the shrewdest and most competent critic of his day with the Mr Casaubon of the novel, with his absurd Key to all Mythologies', and Mr Gordon Haight, the editor of George Eliot's letters, evidently regards any resemblances between them as purely coincidental.

Of course, to talk about 'identification' is to oversimplify. 'Was Mark Pattison Mr Casaubon?' is a question too crude to deserve an answer; creative artists are not photographers. But it is reasonable to ask: How far did George Eliot's creation in fact resemble the living man? And how far was George Eliot, whatever she intended, aware of the resemblance?

The likeness was close enough at several points. Casaubon devoted his life to the production of a work of scholarship that never saw the light of day. You may remember his physical appearance—an unattractive creature, sandy-haired, sallow-faced, 'with two white moles with hairs on them', with 'a bitterness in the mouth and a venom in the glance', whose protestations of love were like 'the cawings of an amorous rook'. You will recall that this 'dried preparation', this 'lifeless embalment of knowledge', 'no better than a mummy', married a high-minded, warm-hearted, impulsive girl, twenty-seven years younger than himself, 'given to self-mortification', and worshipping an ideal of learning that she believed to be embodied in her husband, who (she hoped) would provide her with the key to an intellectual paradise: 'It would be like marrying Pascal, I should learn to see the truth by the same light as great men have seen it by.' *Middlemarch* tells the story of Dorothea's disillusionment, how she discovered the emptiness of her husband's intellect and the pettiness and coldness of his nature.

This literary picture was given to the world in 1872,[1] just ten years after Pattison was elected Rector of Lincoln and married Francis Strong. It resembles him in three respects:

[1] *Middlemarch* was published in monthly parts between December 1871 and December 1872.

the nature of his work, his personal appearance, and the circumstances of his marriage. Pattison was already celebrated for his learning, and he was known to be engaged upon a biography of Isaac Casaubon. As for his appearance: 'With his long hooked nose, sparse beard, and withered skin' said one observer, 'he always reminded me of a Rembrandt etching'; another likened him to a bird of prey. He had been married for ten years to a wife who, like Dorothea, was twenty-seven years younger than her husband—he was practically forty-eight when they were married and she twenty-one—a high-minded and warm-hearted young woman, with a strong leaning to High Church asceticism—as a girl, we are told, she would secretly 'do penance for the smallest fault, imaginary or real, by lying for hours on the bare floor or the stones, with her arms in the attitude of the cross'—and she venerated scholarship, which she saw embodied in her husband. Years later, when she herself had made a name in the criticism of art, and friends urged her not to sacrifice her own health to his well-being, she replied, 'If one life is to give way to the other, I feel sure it should be mine; his is worth much more. I think he is the only truly learned man I know.'

The full history of that marriage has never been written; but, as we shall see, it went wrong, like the Casaubons' marriage, almost from the first; and, though appearances were kept up, the bitterness below the surface cannot have escaped an observer of ordinary shrewdness. It did not escape Lord Rosebery: 'The secret of his character', he wrote, 'cannot well be published, for I presume that in his case his relations to Mrs Pattison gave the key?...I remember him about 1866 looking wizened and wintry by the side of his blooming wife.'

Plainly, the resemblances between the Casaubons and the Pattisons were striking; but so were the points of difference, especially between the husbands. In Dorothea Casaubon, there were blanks, as it were, that are filled up by Francis Pattison, but there is nothing in the fictional portrait that contradicts the reality; the innocent and high-minded girl in the book might have grown into the brilliant and versatile woman of real life. The essential attributes of Dorothea—the religious temperament, the warmth of human sympathy, the desire to improve other people and the conditions of other people's lives, the worship of learning and 'mental culture'—were all of them to be found in Francis Pattison; it was only in inessentials that the two women differed.

Mr Casaubon presents a more difficult problem: the prematurely aged appearance, the stilted utterance, the selfishness about the larger things in life, the meanness about the little ones ('Mr Casaubon was liable to think that others were providentially made for him')—these traits Pattison and Casaubon had in common. And, whether or not she was copying from the life, George Eliot describes Casaubon as suffering from a defect that made Pattison unhappy all his days: the inability to communicate the affection that he felt and to evoke the affection that he needed. But the ruling passion of life for both of them was the love of learning; and here George Eliot if she meant her picture to be taken for Mark Pattison did him a grave injustice: for while Pattison was 'a truly learned man' and a 'master mind', his counterpart in *Middlemarch* was a commonplace pedant whose life-work was a sham.

The really interesting question that arises from this confrontation of fiction and reality is not whether George Eliot 'meant' Mr Casaubon to 'be' Mark Pattison—those are words capable of many shades of meaning—it is, more precisely, this: whatever her intentions were, could she conceivably have been unaware of the resemblances between the couple she created on the one hand and the Rector and Mrs Pattison on the other? And, if she was aware of those resemblances, must she not have known full well when she published her novel that many of her readers would believe that the pictures were meant to be taken for portraits?

To these questions, I think, there can only be one answer. By whatever process of suggestion the two characters came into being in George Eliot's mind, and whatever other sources she drew upon when she created them,[1] she cannot have doubted that they would be identified by most of her informed readers with the Rector

---

[1] I do not say that the idea of Mr Casaubon was first presented to George Eliot by the figure of Mark Pattison. Mrs Joan Bennett has suggested to me, very plausibly, that 'already before 1861 George Eliot had in her mind the pathetic accumulation of fruitless knowledge as a lonely man's substitute for human relations', referring to the second chapter of *Silas Marner*, where the novelist suggests an analogue for the weaver's miserliness: 'The same sort of process has perhaps been undergone by wiser men, when they have been cut off from faith and love—only, instead of a loom and a heap of guineas, they have had some erudite research, some ingenious project, or some well-knit theory.'

of Lincoln and his wife. For anyone who was inclined to question the identification, it would surely have been clinched by the name 'Casaubon'.

And the identification was the more certain to be made because George Eliot was known to be on terms of friendship, even of intimacy, with the Pattisons. It was not a case where the writer accused of a deliberate libel could reply 'But I cannot have had you in mind, I did not even know of your existence'; quite the reverse. Mrs Pattison was a frequent visitor at the Lewes's house in Regent's Park while *Middlemarch* was being written, and George Eliot actually visited Lincoln College in 1870. It is plain from her recently published letters that the older woman became the confidant of the unhappy young wife, whose marriage had already gone gravely wrong. According to Sir Charles Dilke, to whom Mrs Pattison must surely have recounted all the circumstances of her earlier marriage, a number of passages in more intimate letters, now destroyed, are practically repeated in George Eliot's account of Dorothea as a girl: 'Dorothea's reference to her marriage to Casaubon and Casaubon's account of his marriage to Dorothea' are, says Dilke, 'as a fact given by the novelist almost in Mark Pattison's words' and 'the religious side of Dorothea Brooke was taken by George Eliot from the letters of Mrs Pattison.'[1]

---

[1] Mrs Humphry Ward gives us a glimpse of George Eliot in Oxford; she was present as a girl when George Eliot visited the Pattisons at Lincoln, a year before *Middlemarch* began its serial publication:

'As we turned into the quadrangle of Lincoln, suddenly, at one of the upper windows of the Rector's lodgings, which occupied the far right-hand corner of the quad, there appeared the head and shoulders of Mrs Pattison, as she looked out and beckoned smiling to Mrs

George Eliot, then, must surely have known that her pictures would be generally taken to be portraits, and, what is more, that they would be recognized by the supposed originals themselves. And this suggests a more interesting question: George Eliot was a writer who specialized in knowledge of the human emotions; can she have failed to know how deep a wound she would inflict upon the Rector by the 'pitiless ridicule' (the phrase is Leslie Stephen's) with which she drew her cruel picture of a pedant 'without heart or brain'? And how could she justify such treatment of a person with whom she was, outwardly at least, on terms of friendship?

Perhaps it is a sufficient answer to say that friendship must be sacrificed to the high purposes of art. Strangely enough, in this case the friendship survived; at any rate, there seems to have been no break in the relations between the Pattisons and the Leweses, and a later entry in the Rector's diary shows that *Middlemarch* was one of the books from which he gave private 'readings' in his study to his female disciples.

Lewes. It was a brilliant apparition, as though a French portrait by Greuze or Perronneau had suddenly slipped into a vacant space in the old college wall. The pale, pretty head, *blond cendrée*, the delicate smiling features and white throat; a touch of black, a touch of blue; a white dress; a general eighteenth century impression as though of powder and patches: Mrs Lewes perceived it in a flash, and I saw her run eagerly to Mr Lewes and draw his attention to the window and its occupant. She took his arm, while she looked and waved...I seemed to see her consciously and deliberately committing [the scene] to memory.'

It cannot, however, have been on this occasion that George Eliot first conceived the character of Dorothea; *Middlemarch* must have been well under way by this time.

It has been suggested by admirers of George Eliot that the continuance of their friendly relations affords a proof that neither the novelist nor either 'victim' was aware of the supposed identification, and Mr Gordon Haight makes light of the whole affair: 'The only real fact of resemblance', he says, 'is that both Dorothea and Mrs Pattison were 27 years younger than their husbands.' Even if there was a closer resemblance, he argues, the survival of the friendship proves that the Pattisons cannot have noticed it.

I think we must look a little deeper than this. According to Sir Charles Dilke, Mrs Pattison professed never to have read *Middlemarch* (though he admits that a letter that came to light after her death shows clearly that she must have done so) and it was an offence to mention the book in her presence. There can only, I think, be one explanation of why she adopted this disingenuous attitude: she knew that George Eliot had reproduced—indeed, had practically quoted—her matrimonial confidences. She may have forgiven the novelist for taking this liberty; she may have sanctioned or actually encouraged it; she may even have felt grateful for the sympathetic literary presentation of her case. But in public she had to deny that she had read the book if she was to avoid being drawn into discussions in the course of which she might have been forced either to make embarrassing admissions or to tell actual untruths.

As for the Rector, George Eliot—the confidant of the suffering wife—must have meant to make him suffer in his turn, and she was shrewd enough to know that she could do so safely: Pattison was not so vain as to be blind to the odious resemblance, but he was too proud to admit by any public gesture that a resemblance existed. He had to endure seeing his own stilted proposal of marriage reproduced almost word for word and held up to ridicule, in the knowledge that his wife had repeated it *verbatim* to her friend the novelist. George Eliot could be sure both that he would suffer and that he would suffer in silence. The story, in fact, is of strong action by one high-minded woman on behalf of another.

Now I should like to call attention to two remarkable coincidences. If art imitates life, life, it has been observed, takes its revenge by imitating art. There are further parallels in this case between the fact and the fiction— parallels that George Eliot could not have been aware of, except prophetically, when she wrote her novel.

Dorothea Casaubon found consolation for her husband's lack of sympathy in a romantic attachment, formed before his death, to a man whom she married when she became a widow. Three years after *Middlemarch* was published, Sir Charles Dilke, who had known Mrs Pattison slightly as a girl, resumed his friendship with her; he then played in her life a *rôle* exactly corresponding with the part played in *Middlemarch* by Will Ladislaw—a romantic friendship was followed, after the death of the detested husband, by marriage to the widow.

Life imitated art again when Pattison died. Shortly after Casaubon's death, you will remember, Dorothea was informed of a sinister codicil to his will. The discovery shook her painfully: her world (I quote the words of the novel) 'was in a state of convulsive change. One change terrified her as if it had been a sin; it was a violent shock of repulsion from her departed husband, who had had hidden thoughts.' The day after Pattison died, his widow underwent a similar experience: she discovered a codicil to his will, the truth about which she supposed he had concealed from her, and the discovery wounded her and stirred her to bitter indignation: 'It is inexpressibly painful', she wrote, 'to think he was deliberately lying and to have these hideous thoughts to keep us company to his grave.' Her suspicions of her husband were, I think, unfounded; it is none the less remarkable that in real life, as in the novel, a widow was violently affected by the discovery, in a codicil to his will, of her husband's 'hidden thoughts'.

I cannot part from *Belinda* and *Middlemarch* without referring to an amusing skit that plays upon the two novels by a neglected author, Andrew Lang. In the late 1880s Lang contributed to *The St James's Gazette* a series of 'Essays in Epistolary Parody'; they were collected in a volume called *Old Friends*, and published, with a dedication to Rhoda Broughton herself, in 1890. Lang's formula is the imaginary exchange of letters between characters figuring in different books. One of these 'essays' consists of a correspondence between Professor Forth and Mr Casaubon and their respective wives. The learned husbands arrange to attend a philological conference in Cambridge; Mrs Forth takes the opportunity of making an assignation with her old suitor David Rivers in Magdalen

Grove, while Mrs Casaubon contrives that Ladislaw shall be invited to lecture at the Mechanics Institute in Middlemarch (his subject is 'The Immutability of Morals'), and she induces him to take advantage of the occasion and to cheer her solitude with a reading of the earlier sonnets in Dante's *Vita Nuova*—'We have no books of poetry here', she piteously tells him, 'except a Lithuanian translation of the Rig Veda'. The atmosphere of the Casaubon household and the high-mindedness of its mistress are very faithfully reproduced.

My third portrait of Pattison is deeper and truer, because more sympathetic, than either Rhoda Broughton's or George Eliot's; it was drawn by Mrs Humphry Ward in *Robert Elsmere*. Mrs Ward knew Pattison in the 1860s when her father, Matthew Arnold's brother Tom, brought her to live in Oxford as a girl in her teens. The Rector was kind to her and encouraged her in her studies: 'Get to the bottom of something', he told her, 'choose a subject, and know *everything* about it!'

Robert Elsmere came out in 1888, four years after Pattison's death. The book created an immediate sensation; in the year it was published, it went through twenty editions, and it sold about half a million copies in America. Twenty years later, 100,000 copies of a cheap edition were sold in a year.

It is not, perhaps, a book to be read today entirely for pleasure; it is long and heavy, and its author, though like George Eliot she had a message to deliver, was not intended by Nature for a novelist; and though she thought hard and read much and felt seriously, she lacked George Eliot's shrewdness and her gift for moral epigram.

None the less, *Robert Elsmere* is an important social document of its period. Its subject is the undermining of orthodox Christian belief by the Higher Criticism and scientific inquiry, and the consequent 'dissociation of the moral judgment from a special series of religious formulae which is the crucial, the epoch-making fact of our day'; the theme is illustrated by the story of a young clergyman who, under the influence of a learned and cynical old sceptic, loses his faith and renounces his Orders, and so creates a gulf between himself and his devout young wife.

The book ranges over the Westmorland fells, a Surrey parish, and the West End of London; but it is permeated by Oxford, and in particular by the high-minded liberal religious seriousness of T. H. Green; it is dedicated to Green's memory, and extended passages from his lay sermons are incorporated in the text.

Robert Elsmere contains several Oxford portraits. T. H. Green appears as Mr Grey, 'that great son of modern Oxford'; there are traits of Walter Pater, as well as of Amiel, in Mr Langham, the Epicurean—'Am I a corrupter of youth?' he asks himself after lending an undergraduate a copy of Senancourt—and Mark Pattison appears as the Squire of Murewell, Roger Wendover (like George Eliot, Mrs Ward labelled her portrait with a scholarly name). It is the squire, with his encyclopaedic library, full of the tools of rationalist inquiry, and his searching criticisms of the foundations of belief, who undermines the basis of Elsmere's life and faith.

Mrs Ward disguised her likeness: she transported her subject from Oxford and made him a rich and lonely old bachelor, who had dedicated his life to learning, inhabiting an ancestral Hall surrounded by a magnificent library and priceless works of art. But the physical characteristics, down to the mannerisms of speech, are unmistakable: the 'harsh face', with its brown wrinkles; the long hooked nose, the thin bony fingers, the sarcastic gleam of the eyes. Like Pattison, who nearly followed Newman to Rome, Roger Wendover 'was one of them in 45', and he spent ten years in Germany, where he 'buried his last chance of living like other men'; and like Pattison, he devoted his life to preparing a book that was never published.

But there is this great difference between Roger Wendover on the one hand and Mr Casaubon and Professor Forth on the other, as presentations of Mark Pattison: with Mrs Ward's character, unlike Rhoda Broughton's and George Eliot's, the nearer you get to the centre of it, the closer is the resemblance to the real man. The bent and cast of Wendover's mind, his rationalism, his anti-clericalism, his mordant cynicism, his encyclopaedic learning—all these reproduce attributes of Pattison that have been transmitted to us by those who knew him. And the titles she chose for the Squire's books—his two *parerga, Idols of the Market-place* and *Essays on English Culture,* and his great, unfinished, *History of Human Testimony*—these are Mrs Ward's witty comments on the books that Pattison might well have written, but never wrote.

Mrs Ward saw into her subject at least as deeply as George Eliot: she knew that the man she had chosen to portray was 'sick in mind and sick in soul, for all his book learning'; that he was 'made awkward and unapproachable by the slightest touch of personal sympathy'; and she endowed the Squire of Murewell with a secret that he shared with Pattison—a 'dark consciousness of inherited fatality'; it transpires that his father has killed himself in a fit of hereditary madness: 'So that', one of her characters exclaims, 'is the skeleton in this very magnificent cupboard!' In his own cupboard, as we shall see, Pattison had just such a skeleton himself.

If Mrs Ward is as penetrating as George Eliot, she is more sympathetic. 'He has a heart, he has!' exclaims the devoted family doctor, for whom the Squire feels nothing but a faintly affectionate contempt. And Elsmere himself, when he takes his last leave of the old cynic who has destroyed his faith and dislocated his life, and now lies before him on his deathbed, 'bent down and kissed the Squire's forehead tenderly, as a son might have done'. Pattison inspired just such devotion in those of his pupils who felt the power of his personality and discerned its pathos.

Mrs Ward disclaimed any attempt at portraiture, admitting only 'a likeness in outward aspect, a few personal traits, and the two main facts of great learning and a general impatience of fools'; but in Roger Wendover she left the fullest and most sympathetic presentation of Pattison that has come down to us.

I have given examples of the impression that Mark Pattison made on other people. In his *Memoirs* he painted his own portrait.

The book was published in 1885, a year after Pattison's death. He wrote it, partly in his own hand, partly by dictation, in his study at Lincoln during the last months of 1883, when he knew himself to be in the grip of the disease that killed him in the following summer, and we can follow its progress almost day by day in his diaries and his correspondence:

Here the daily record was broken off [he writes] by my becoming too ill to continue it. I got weaker daily, till the weakness itself became such pain I would fain have got ease by dying. I thought myself dying, those about me thought so, and Dr Tuckwell told me in plain words that I could not get well. I fairly stood face to face with death, and was content. All business dispositions had been made, and I proceeded now to the arrangement of my papers...These preparations made, I resigned myself to the inevitable. In order to have some occupation which did not require reference to books, I began to dictate my memoirs, and brought them down to 1860.

To a friend who wrote asking for a photograph he replied, 'I have done with photos and am giving the few ounces of blood which remain in my body and brain to the written photo of myself which I pompously call my "Memoir".'

Pattison's written photograph was, in the opinion of Mr Gladstone, 'among the most tragic and the most memorable books of the nineteenth century'. It is a bleak production, without grace of style and merciless in its introspection. Pattison never wrote to please; he used an inelegant unornamented prose, and his rare excursions into metaphor were apt to be unhappy. 'Even at this day', he could write, 'a country squire or rector, on landing with his cub under his wing in Oxford, finds himself much at sea as to the respective advantages or demerits of the various colleges.' Nor does he seek to entertain the readers with picturesque reminiscences: 'I have really no history', he says on the first page, 'but a mental history.'

The *Memoirs*, however, do not consist entirely of introspection; they introduce us to the young man whom Mrs Ward and George Eliot and Rhoda Broughton never met, but who grew up to be Roger Wendover and Mr Casaubon and Professor Forth, and they give us some vivid glimpses of his early life and surroundings.

He describes himself in the Yorkshire home of his childhood, 'wandering over the moor whole days, haunting the skirts of the woods at night, on the look-out for birds and moths', absorbing 'the sense of the country', feeling 'a delight in rural objects'. He was already a student: 'I read enormously...ten times as much as I remembered; what is more odd, I read far more than I ever took in the sense of as I read it. I think the mechanical act of perusal must have given me a sort of pleasure. Books, as books, irrespective of their contents, were my delight.'

We see him as a freshman, in his first term at Oriel, a lanky, awkward, 'bumpkin' of eighteen meeting the head of his college in the street, and cutting him out of sheer nervousness—'I saw he knew me and smiled, and I tortured myself with conjecture as to what the smile meant—contempt or compassion'—and we are present at his first, disastrous, wine-party:

Oh, the icy coldness, the dreary Egyptian blankness of that 'wine'; the guests slipped away one by one under pretext of engagements, and I was left alone with an almost untouched dessert, to be carried off as perquisite by the college scout. It was long before I summoned courage to give a repetition of the entertainment. I thought I was ostracised, black-balled, expelled from society; I reflected hopelessly on the causes of the breakdown, ascribing it to every cause except the simple one—clownishness and want of the *usage du monde*.

If Pattison felt awkward among strange undergraduates, he was hardly more at ease with a companion of his own choice; here is his description of his relations with a friend who was staying with him at Hauxwell in his holidays:

I used to retire every morning to my own little bedroom, where I had established my books, and which was the only corner of the house I could use as a study. Solitude was necessary to me; I had not—I have never had—the power of commanding my attention properly in the presence of another human being, and at this date the power of the will over the attention was remarkably feeble. ——, sociable even in his reading hours, would come in occasionally with his book, and at last established himself there to keep me company. Good-natured creature as he was, and some years older than me, I did not know how to tell him that he put me out. Being then totally destitute of tact, I tried to effect my end by being morose and disagreeable. I succeeded at last, and he retired to his own room, which, as the stranger's bedroom, was a much better one than mine. I had gained my point, but, as so often since, with the uncomfortable consciousness of having done so in a wrong way. I mention this trifling incident because it is typical of my way of doing things all my life.

Pattison traces the outline of his career, with a few touches of colour like those I have just quoted, through his time as an undergraduate at Oriel and as a junior Fellow of

Lincoln, doing full justice to the crisis of his life, when he came within an ace of being elected Rector in 1851. His account of that episode has become part of Oxford history, a classic example of academical intrigue.

But he breaks off the story of his life, if he can be said to tell it as a story, just before 1861, the turning point of his career, the year in which he married and finally obtained the headship of his college; of the events of the last twenty-five years he tells us nothing.

The *Memoirs*, it will be seen, are complementary to the portraits of Pattison drawn by the novelists: they fill up two *lacunae* that were perforce left blank by observers who knew him only in later life, and then knew only the front that he presented to the world: first, they tell us something of his early years, of the conditions that helped to make him what he became; then, they admit us to his study, where his real life was lived, and recount the history of his mind. They are his posthumous answer to the crude injustice done him by Rhoda Broughton's cardboard caricature and to the deeper injury done him by a greater novelist.

The main purpose of the book was not to tell the story of its author's life, but to describe his intellectual development. The record involves some account of his writings, but his allusions to these are almost casual. For to him his books, whether those he planned or those he actually completed, were merely the by-products of a life of study. His published works—the Casaubon, the Life of Milton, and the occasional essays and reviews, of which only a small proportion were included in the two volumes published after his death—give an indication, but only an indication, of the range and the depth of his explorations in the world of ideas. The *Memoirs* tell us of the more ambitious projects that he formed and then, one after another, laid aside: a history of 'the laws of the progress of thought in modern Europe' was cut down to a history of thought in the eighteenth century, and then abandoned, having been forestalled by Leslie Stephen. 'A scientific history of the self-development of theological opinion' was given up because he found, from the reception of his contribution to *Essays and Reviews*, that there was no informed and impartial public in England for a theological work. He turned to a topic that had attracted him from a very early time, the history of scholarship. 'My first scheme', he says, 'was to write the history of learning from the Renaissance downwards.' But 'one's ambition is always in inverse proportion to one's knowledge', and he soon contracted his aim to scholarship in France. Of this plan his book on Casaubon was the first-fruits; his work on Scaliger was to be a further and more elaborate instalment.

It would have been no mere biography, but a survey of the world of learning in Scaliger's time, and he spent (he says) nearly thirty years in getting together the material for it. 'In the autumn of 1883', he writes, 'I returned from the Tyrol with the full purpose of devoting the next twelve months to complete the composition...when I was struck down by the malady which has cut off all hope of my ever being able to execute this or any other literary scheme.' 'I have gathered with infinite pains the material for my great work, but this will all be wasted, for I shall not live to finish it, and no one else can find the clue.'

The great work never appeared. But Pattison would not have admitted that his life had therefore been a wasted one; the real fruit of learning is, as he himself declared, 'not a book, but a man'; his own life's work was his life; if he had been asked what he had to show for half a century's devotion to learning, he might have answered, without vanity, that he had himself to show for it.

Learning did not mean for him the accumulation of knowledge, any more than it meant the publication of books; it meant understanding, in detail and in depth, the universe around one, as revealed by the researches of scientists and historians; in a word, it meant a securely based philosophy. And since Pattison's philosophical convictions came gradually to be more and more at variance with the creed in which he had been nurtured, the history of his intellectual development was also the history of his religious opinions.

In this respect his *Memoirs* inevitably provoke a comparison with the account that Newman had given to the world twenty years before of his own spiritual *Aeneid*. In each case the style seems peculiarly unsuited to the message: Newman urges persuasively, in his own firm but gentle speaking voice, the case for intellectual rigidity; Pattison's account of reason as something alive, changing and developing continually, both in the individual mind and in the world at large, is conveyed in a harsh, angular diction, without sentiment or grace of style.

Each book in its own way compels one to respect the sincerity of its author.

I have changed in many things; [wrote Newman] in this I have not. From the age of fifteen dogma has been the fundamental principle of my religion; I know no other religion. I cannot enter into the idea of any other sort of religion; religion, as a mere sentiment, is to me a dream and a mockery. As well can there be filial love without the fact of a father, as devotion without the fact of a Supreme Being. What I held in 1816 I held in 1833, and I hold in 1864. Please God I shall hold it to the end.

Pattison, in the closing pages of his *Memoirs*, sums up in very different language a very different mental history.

Slowly, [he writes] and not without laborious effort, I began to emerge, to conquer, as it were, in the realm of ideas. It was all growth, development, and I have never ceased to grow, to develop, to discover, up to the very last...Slow as the steps were, they have all been forward. I seemed to my friends to have changed, to have gone over from High Anglicanism to Latitudinarianism, or Rationalism, or Unbelief or whatever the term may be. This is not so; what took place with me was simple expansion of knowledge and ideas. To my home Puritan religion, almost narrowed to two points—fear of God's wrath and faith in the doctrine of the atonement—the idea of the Church was a widening of the horizon which stirred up the spirit and filled it with enthusiasm. The notion of the Church soon expanded itself beyond the limits of the Anglican communion and became the wider idea of the Catholic Church. Then Anglicanism fell off from me, like an old garment, as Puritanism had done before.

Now the idea of the Catholic Church is only a mode of conceiving the dealings of divine Providence with the whole race of mankind. Reflection on the history and condition of humanity, taken as a whole, gradually convinced me that this theory of the relation of all living beings to the Supreme Being was too narrow and inadequate. So I passed out of the Catholic phase, but slowly, and in many years, to that highest development when all religions appear in their historical light, as efforts of the human spirit to come to an understanding with that Unseen Power whose pressure it feels, but whose motives are a riddle. Thus Catholicism dropped off me as another husk which I had outgrown. There was no conversion or change of view: I could no more have helped what took place within me than I could have helped becoming ten years older.

The same evolution [he proceeds] which thus worked out my conception of the supreme law of the universe prevailed in all the subordinate branches of investigation through which my studies led me...It was thus, e.g. that I arrived at last at the idea of a University.

How Pattison's experience altered his intellectual standpoint, and with it his idea of what a university should be, is the theme—in so far as it has a single theme—of the lectures that make up this book.

Note. No account of 'Pattison and the Novelists' would be complete without a reference to Robert Liddell's *The Almond Tree*. This novel, which was published by Messrs Cape in 1938 and has long been out of print, is an imaginative recreation of the last years of Pattison's life, seen through the eyes of the three principal characters. The author was for some time on the staff of the Bodleian Library, where he must have familiarized himself with the Pattison papers, and his novel may be described as a dramatization of the letters of Pattison, Mrs Pattison, and Meta Bradley; he has altered the setting (Pattison, for instance, becomes Dr Paul Ramus, Head Master of a school for boys) and invented plenty of supporting detail; but the characters and the story are taken straight from life, and the language at innumerable points repeats *verbatim* that of the original letters. The resulting book, however, is not a piece of plagiarism or mere reporting but a creative work of considerable psychological insight.

PRIVATE LIFE OF A SCHOLAR

Over against the fictional images of Pattison given to the world by Rhoda Broughton, George Eliot and Mrs Humphry Ward I have set Pattison's presentation of himself—an introspective account, recording how his mind developed, and how it became dominated by devotion to an ideal of learning. Judging from these portraits, one might well conclude that Pattison was a man who lived only in his study and felt only for his books.

I want now to give some glimpses of Pattison's personal and private life, drawing upon his diaries and journals and the dozens of volumes containing his correspondence preserved in the Bodleian Library. These documents tell us about his home and his family, about his married life, and about an attachment that meant much to him in his closing years. They reveal him as a human being, very different both from the mummified pedant of *Middlemarch* and from the almost disembodied intellect presented to us in his *Memoirs*.

Let me first say something about his upbringing. Pattison's childhood was spent in the Rectory of the village of Hauxwell in the North Riding of Yorkshire, six or seven miles from Richmond, on the slopes of Wensleydale.

Even now, when Catterick Camp has engulfed most of

the neighbourhood to the north of it, Hauxwell is lonely
enough. A hundred years ago, winter would cut it off
completely from the rest of the world for weeks at a
time. Its total population was about three hundred. Every
day, thirty children would repair to the schoolroom
adjoining the Rectory to be given lessons by the Rector's
daughters. The Gales lived at the Hall, half a mile away.
There is some mention in Pattison's youthful diaries of
partridge-shooting with a Colonel Coore; but gentlemen's houses in the neighbourhood were few and far
between. A mile or two away was The Salutation, the
nearest posting-stage on the Leeming Lane, the high-road
by which, stopping two nights on the way, at Sheffield
and Birmingham, the coach would take you the two
hundred and twenty miles to London.

Here Pattison spent his boyhood until, when he was
nineteen, he went up to Oxford; he was never sent to
school, not even to a day-school. Here he imbibed what
he called 'the sentiment of nature', spending long days on
the rectory farm, getting in the hay, sowing turnips or
gathering potatoes, fishing in the beck, riding alone over
the moors on his pony, or following one or other of the
two local packs of hounds. Here he developed a passion
that never left him—a passion for the countryside, and
especially for the dales and moors.

He was never satisfied, in his feelings either for things or
for people, with mere sensation or sentiment. Even as a
boy he 'rationalized', as he put it, his passion for birds and
moths and butterflies by studying Selby's *Ornithology* and
Rennie on Insects; and he felt that his own love of land-

scape was imperfect until he had given it an 'intellectual foundation' in geology. But, rationalize it as he might, love of his native place sank deep into his heart. On his last visit to Wensleydale, not long before his death, he described in his diary a walk along the bank of the stream where so often, in boyhood and later manhood, he had spent solitary days of trout-fishing. 'Most enjoyable', he noted; then he added:

Yet withal the δεῖγμα προστατήριον καρδίας τερασκόπου is underneath all—a pain which mounts at moments to agony— the thought that this is slipping from me, that this is the last time, that even now it is only a phantasm of what once was but is not, the pang of a yearning heart, which nothing but affection can satisfy—and this dale with its reminiscences is the shell in which home love once was, and *is* no longer. It may be this is 'only sentimental'; if it is, then sentiment is the source of the keenest pain I can experience.

The inner shell of 'home love' was the Rectory where his parents lived with their twelve children: Mark himself, born in 1813, then ten sisters, then Frank, the youngest, born in 1834.

The house was a small one. I visited it more than once before it was pulled down a year or two ago, and I found it hard to believe that the Rectory could ever have accommodated a family of fourteen, with all its servants.

The Rector of Hauxwell came from Devonshire; he was born before the end of the eighteenth century, and was proud of having been up at Brasenose when it was still the first College in Oxford. In 1812, when he was twenty-four, he married a fatherless girl of nineteen, the only child and heiress of a prosperous Yorkshire banker named Winn.

Mrs Pattison appears in the family correspondence as a pale and pious shadow; his father's was the figure that dominated Mark's early years.

Mr Pattison was devoted to his eldest child. He taught him as much elementary Classics as was needed to get him to Oxford, and eagerly followed his doings at the University; he wrote letters almost every week (they are all in the Bodleian) to 'My very very dear boy', and made no difficulty about paying the undergraduate's modest bills. When Mark got only a second in the Schools, his father took it very well, and when he heard of Mark's election to a fellowship at Lincoln, in 1839, he wept with joy.

Then, in the early 'forties, Mr Pattison turned against his son, and during the remaining twenty-five years of his life he never, so far as I can discover, wrote him another letter. The immediate reason for this was a religious difference: the Rector of Hauxwell was an Evangelical; the young Mark at Oxford was subjected to the first onset of Tractarianism; the father could not forgive his son for yielding to the influence of Pusey and Newman. But the violence of the father's reaction was due to something deeper. Several years before Mark fell under the Tractarian influence, in the summer of 1834, Mr Pattison had had to be removed from Hauxwell and lodged for some months in a private lunatic asylum at Acomb near York. Lunatic asylums, in those days, were not very comfortable places; and Acomb was described by Mr Pattison as 'the most nauseous den to which a clergyman of the Established

Church, and that clergyman a gentleman, could have been consigned'. For some time after his release, the Rector's mind was still so deeply deranged, and his feelings against his wife and family were so violent, that it was not thought safe for him to return to Hauxwell, and Mark gave up the whole of the Lent Term in 1835 in order to be with his father in a lodging-house in York—an experience that must surely have made a lasting impression on the mind of a third-year undergraduate. In March Mr Pattison returned home, nominally 'cured', to live for thirty years a raging domestic tyrant. One can gather from his daughters' letters what life in the Rectory was like. When the black mood was on him, the Rector would lock himself up in his room for days on end, taking his meals alone and refusing to have any communication with his children, except to burst out and rant against them or to spit in their faces. On one stormy occasion he flung a dish at his wife; on another, he locked the village children out of the schoolroom and forbade his daughters to instruct them. He would preach against his family before the parishioners in the little village church: 'They will bring down my gray hairs in sorrow to the grave', and when visitors came to the Rectory he would ask them, 'Will you take your dinner with the Papists in the dining room, or with the poor persecuted Protestant here?'

It was an *idée fixe* with him that none of his daughters should marry; they must all stay at home and keep the family and the family fortune together. Two daughters dared to break this inhibition: Eleanor married a neighbouring clergyman; Rachel, a yeoman farmer. Mr Pattison tried to persuade Eleanor's father-in-law to withhold his consent by telling him that there was insanity in the Pattison family; failing in this aim, on the day of the wedding he locked himself up, in protest, in the hay-loft. Since he could not prevent them from marrying, Mr Pattison put pressure on his wife to disinherit the disobedient daughters. Under her marriage settlement her fortune was on her death to be divided equally between her children unless she appointed otherwise by deed or will. Mrs Pattison steadfastly refused to execute any disposition discriminating between her children: they should all share equally in what she had to leave. Of course this infuriated her husband. His opportunity arrived when, in 1860, she was on her deathbed: she asked him for the sacrament, and he refused to give it unless she complied with his demand about her will. She died unshriven.

Mr Pattison himself died five years later, in 1865. By his will he disinherited his married daughters and (except for a small devise of land) his sons.

When the news reached Pattison, he had recourse to Latin in order to record it in his Diary. Two words of comment were enough: 'Deus misereatur!' He meant, no doubt, that his father's soul stood in need of divine mercy, not that he hoped or believed that such mercy would be extended to it—'divine mercy' had in any case for long been to him a phrase without significance—for he went on to call the dead man 'homo morosus et perfidiosus' and to stigmatize his will as 'iniquissimum'.

When people (especially young people) do wrong things nowadays, it is often suggested by way of explanation or excuse that they must have come from a 'divided' or unhappy home. If we are inclined to pass judgement upon Mark Pattison for his faults of temper we might with at least equal justice remember the skeleton in his domestic cupboard.

For nearly thirty years the hostility of the family tyrant made it impossible for the eldest son to pay any but short and unhappy visits to his home. But his father could not prevent his sisters from corresponding with him (though they never dared to give him letters to deliver to the post at Richmond, for fear they would 'find their way into the beck') and the elder girls wrote to him several times a week for many years. They adored their brother: he was their oracle, their example, their idol. They were pious and intelligent girls, always anxious to improve themselves; Mark directed their studies from a distance. During their Tractarian period he prescribed religious reading for the eldest four girls, for whom he took the place of a parent; and Eleanor, his second, and for long his favourite, sister, taught herself Latin and Greek under his instruction.

Mr Pattison had his temperate intervals, and from time to time he permitted one or other of his daughters to pay Mark a visit; a letter from Rachel, written in 1859, gives a good idea of the relations between the sisters in the country rectory and their Oxford brother:

... It is her [Dora's] first visit to O[xford]; she goes wiser than I did in 1847—how raw I felt then—I conjecture it will be very sober steady lionizing you will take—walking her into a Quad

—but don't leave her in doubt what it is—it puzzled me so—
you don't know what a country life begets in a mind. You
can't fancy how new the commonest things are—things which
are to you like what trees & birds are to us, you used to tell me
in '54 I had no eyes and sometimes I felt it so, I was so bewildered.
Why do I tell you all this? It is only because I have been full of
O[xford] all day—I see you step across yr room I often think I
never saw you walk so but in O[xford] I felt I was in your
home when I saw that step, in that home which had combined
to form you—it was so elastic—so vigorous so characteristic &
then all the furniture the arrangements the mantelpiece—oh it
was so real O & that night you went out to dinner & came back
& told me you could not get away before...oh how I wished
I was different, fit to be there—I did detest myself—well you &
D[ora] will be there now sitting on that sofa near the window...

These were rare escapes for the Pattison girls. Their life
at Hauxwell was punctuated by tragic episodes. In 1844
Grace, the fifth daughter, died of consumption at the age
of twenty-two—one of the sisters described her 'trembling
on her death bed to see her father enter the room and
shaking with terror at the distant sounds of tumult that
reached her bed'. In 1862 Fanny's mind gave way; she
became obsessed by a delusion of her own 'impurity', and
had to be lodged for a time, like her father, in an asylum.
There were times when things got so bad that the sisters
appealed to Mark, asking whether if they left the house
they had any legal claim upon their father for support.
His answer was that they had no alternative but to stay at
home and stick it out to the end.

As the years went by, Mark's attitude to his sisters became colder and more distant. 'Too long a sacrifice can
make a stone of the heart'—one is reminded of Yeats's

words, but they do not quite fit his case. He certainly had suffered from his father's hostility, but he had suffered at a distance; and though he had been a dutiful brother, he had not really been called upon to make any considerable sacrifice for his sisters. As the years went by his affection for them—never, perhaps, as strong as theirs for him—began to wane; he ceased to share their Tractarian enthusiasm of the 'forties; while they grew up into pious orthodoxy he became rationalist and fiercely anti-clerical; his sympathy hardened into pity; and the death of the tyrant in 1865 broke what must by then have been the only bond between them, except their memories of a common childhood.

The only sister of whom he really continued to be fond was Rachel. When she died in 1874 he wrote in his Diary, 'Bitter! bitter! What is the loss of friends? I never knew what till now', and on the day of the funeral he added, 'My heart has been in Wensleydale since Sunday... My world is half perished in her loss.'

Four years later Rachel was followed to the grave by the most remarkable of the sisters, Dorothy. Dorothy had broken away from home before her father's death to become a village school teacher; she joined an Anglican sisterhood and went to manage a fever hospital at Walsall in Staffordshire; the strength of her character and her supposedly miraculous powers made her a legend, like Florence Nightingale, that lasted long in the Black Country—my nurse, who came from the district, used to tell me stories about her—and the name of 'Sister Dora' was spread over all England after her death by more than one biography.

Pattison admired Dora's brains and character, and despised her for wasting them on piety and nursing. In 1877 he was lecturing in Birmingham; she came up to him when the lecture was over, to be greeted with the words, 'What, Dora, still cutting off little Tommy's fingers and little Jemmy's toes?' A year later she died of cancer, driving the watchers by her bedside out of the room, crying out with her last breath, 'I have lived alone, let me die alone!' The words, perhaps recollected from Keble's *Christian Year*, came strangely from a woman who had spent her whole life among others—in a crowded home, in a religious community, and in the wards of a hospital. When he learned of her death, her brother wrote in his Diary, 'I shall not go to her funeral. I should be sadly out of place among those "Sisters" and long-coated hypocrites.'

Eleanor had been closer to him than any other of his sisters in the early days; a letter from her reached him on his deathbed, asking for 'one last word in memory, at least, of all she had been to him'. In reply, he dictated a message that, according to his wife, was calculated to wound so deeply that she hesitated long before she sent it.

Frances remained devoted to him to the end; but he had lost all affection for her years before: 'her icy reserve [he said] gets on my nerves'. She was in the house when he lay dying; one who was present describes her as 'passionately devoted to him but wholly incapable of showing it in any way', and 'crawling all about the house, a shapeless, speechless, black, body of anguish eaten up with heartache at her own inability to be anything to him'.

Certainly, Pattison did not make it easy for others to feel affection for him, or to show affection if they felt it, But, in order to complete my account of his family relations, I have been forced to anticipate. I return to the year 1861.

That year was an important one in Pattison's life. After a most successful decade as a college tutor, in 1851 he had seen his hopes of becoming head of his college disappointed, and he passed the next ten years in the wilderness—shut up in his college rooms, spending long months of solitary fishing in Yorkshire and Scotland, visiting German universities, lonely and frustrated. Then, in 1861, the tide turned; in January he was elected Rector of Lincoln, and in September he availed himself of the privilege of a head (fellows were still required to be celibate) and married. He was within a month of being forty-eight. I do not think he had ever had any emotional or intimate relationship with the other sex: he hints as much when he tells us in his *Memoirs* that what Marcus Aurelius said of himself—μὴ πρὸ ὥρας ἀνδρωθῆναι—applied to his own case. For his wife, he chose the twenty-one-year-old daughter of a well-known Oxford character, Major Strong, who had retired from the service of the East India Company and was the manager of an Oxford bank. Francis Strong was a very different person from any of her husband's sisters: they dressed in black bombazine; she ordered her fabrics from Liberty. She was strikingly beautiful, very intelligent, deeply religious, emotional, and idealistic. As a girl, she had been a pupil—a rebellious pupil—of Ruskin. Later in life, as Lady Dilke, she became an authority on the history of French art and a leader of the

Women's Trade Union League and other movements for the emancipation of her sex.

Pattison admired her gifts but I do not think that he was in love with her, except in the sense that he counted on her to make him happy. You will remember Mr Casaubon's letter proposing marriage to Dorothea Brooke: it contains in effect Pattison's reasons for proposing marriage to Miss Strong, and I suspect that it echoes the language in which that proposal was put forward.[1] Like Casaubon, Pattison saw in Francis Strong 'an elevation of thought and a capacity for devotedness...adapted to supply aid in graver labours and to cast a charm over vacant hours'. And Miss Strong's reasons for accepting the proposal were, at least in part, like Dorothea's: she married her husband for his mind—and perhaps for his position; it was something, in those days, to be the wife of the head of a college.

Francis Strong certainly provided Pattison with some of the things that he was looking for: according to Mrs Humphry Ward, she brought into his Lodgings 'gaiety, picturesqueness, impatience of the Oxford solemnities and decorums, a sharp, restless wit, and a determination not to

[1] 'Dorothea's defence of her marriage with Casaubon, and Casaubon's account of his marriage to Dorothea in the first book of "Middlemarch", are as a fact given by the novelist almost in Mark Pattison's words' (Sir Charles Dilke, 'Memoir' prefixed to *The Book of the Spiritual Life*, 1905, p. 17). It may be to this statement (for which Lady Dilke was, no doubt, herself the authority) that D. S. MacColl, himself a friend of the Pattisons, refers when he says ('Rhoda Broughton and Emilia Pattison' in *The Nineteenth Century*, CXXXVII, no. 815, January 1945, p. 31), 'There is authority for saying that George Eliot, a friend of both, gave the religious temper of her Dorothea, and reproduced much of the Rector's proposal in Casaubon's letter.'

be academic'. She helped him to create a *salon*, and to fill it with the most 'advanced' people in Oxford and with interesting visitors from the outside world.

Mrs Ward has left a description of the Pattisons' drawing-room; it was 'sparsely furnished with a few old ...mirrors on its white panelled walls, and a Persian carpet with a black centre, on which both the French furniture and the living inmates of the room looked their best'—it evidently displayed the same chaste elegance of taste as Pater's rooms at Brasenose over the way—and she recalls also the Rector in his study, walking up and down, occasionally taking a book from his crowded shelves while Mr Bywater and Mrs Pattison smoked, with the after-luncheon coffee. 'Sometimes (she adds) at a caustic *mot* of Bywater's there would break out the Rector's cackling laugh, which was ugly, no doubt, but when he was amused and at ease, extraordinarily full of mirth.'

Here is the impression of a visitor from Cambridge in the 'seventies, R. C. Jebb:

We have just been sitting in the open air in the court, under the starlight, and Mrs Pattison and I have been smoking her particular cigarettes—made for her in Paris by somebody...She is very difficult to describe...she is very clever: she has tenderness; great courage; and an exquisite sense of humour...she is joyous, and affects a certain specially Oxford type of feminine fastness...she talks of art and books and philosophies...

She appreciated her husband's learning, and, being herself a scholar and competent in many languages, she was able to help him in his work. But she must have been deeply shaken when she discovered how completely lacking he

43

was in religious feeling himself and how utterly unable to sympathize with the religious feelings of others.

Unfortunately, each of them was too good for the other. And since they were both intensely selfish people—his selfishness took the form of self-pity, hers the form of self-righteousness—their marriage was bound to be unhappy.

They were both the victims of ill-health; of the two, he was the more experienced and (if his wife is to be believed) the more resourceful hypochondriac: 'The fainting', she wrote to a friend, 'is always exaggerated, like everything else which can excite commiseration. I have even seen him throw himself down on the landing with great care in similar attacks.' And she went on to suggest, with a glibness that might not have been appreciated by the sufferer himself, that his attacks and 'sick-faint feeling' were to be expected from the nature of his complaint and must 'afford really great relief'.

Husband and wife found a *modus vivendi*: after a serious illness in 1867 Mrs Pattison, on doctor's orders, spent her winters and a large part of her summers alone in a little villa near Nice, working at her art-history, while one of the Rector's nieces kept house for him in the Lodgings at Lincoln. This suited Pattison: he was free from the incubus of his wife's presence, and entitled to complain about her neglect.

We, who see behind the *façade* that, no doubt, concealed the truth from their contemporaries, can imagine how unhappy they must have been together. 'A wall of ice', he wrote in his Diary, 'has been built between us'; the day of his wedding, he says, 'is an anniversary which depresses me to the lowest depths of misery. The heart-pain...lasts for days.'

It is never easy to know for certain why a marriage goes wrong, even if the parties to it themselves think they know the reasons and are ready to explain them, and even if there is plenty of independent testimony to confirm or to correct their explanations. Here, we can only go by our knowledge of the characters involved, and such shreds of evidence as escaped contemporary concealment and have survived the passage of a century.

After Pattison's death, his widow did her best to expunge or excise from his Diaries all references to herself. But a number of passages escaped her; and there reached the Bodleian, nearly fifty years after his death, a series of letters in which he unburdened his feelings to an intimate friend. More revealing are two letters written by Francis Pattison herself that have by chance survived to bear witness against her. She wrote from Nice on 21 January 1876: 'There is one...side of the life with you into which I do not enter, and that is so distasteful to me that the fear of its renewal has often preoccupied me to the exclusion of all other considerations. It is a physical aversion which always existed, though I strove hard to overcome it, and which is now wholly beyond control.'

'You cannot forget', she wrote in a second letter, 'that from the first I expressed the strongest aversion to that side of the common life'—it was not a thing, surely, that a husband was likely to forget—'during 73-4 this became almost insufferable—but I tried to conceal it, hoping that it might settle itself.'

In February 1875, not long before she wrote these letters, Mrs Pattison, while she was staying with friends in Gower Street, received a visit from Sir Charles Dilke. Dilke, whose wife had died six months before, had known Francis Strong fifteen years earlier, when she was an art-student in Kensington and he was little more than a boy. The re-newed friendship ripened quickly: the story is told by Dilke's latest biographer, Mr Roy Jenkins, from the Dilke papers in the British Museum. Soon they began to write to each other regularly at least three times a week, and sometimes, for long periods, every day. Dilke 'asked her advice about almost every difficult decision he had to take'.

Pattison, of course, became aware of this; in 1882 he wrote to an intimate friend, 'She is now quite unsympathetic, reserving all her interest for the other man and his affairs.' How intimate were the relations between Mrs Pattison and Sir Charles, one cannot say; her high-mindedness probably precluded—though she may have felt that it justified—a 'guilty' liaison, and Dilke was seeking his pleasures elsewhere; but it seems plain that they had agreed to marry as soon as circumstances set Mrs Pattison free. In July 1884 the door was opened for their marriage by the Rector's death—and this fact has a bearing on the Crawford divorce case that has not, I think, been re-cognized. That case—which was to be the ruin of Dilke's career—arose out of Mrs Donald Crawford's confession to her husband in the summer of 1885 that she had been guilty of a series of acts of adultery with Sir Charles. The great question in the case was how far Mrs Crawford's confession was to be believed.

According to Mrs Crawford's evidence, her liaison with Dilke ended in the summer of 1884—'in July or August', she said. No one, so far as I know, has called attention to the significance of that date. It was at the end of July in that year that Pattison died; if Dilke was pledged to marry his widow, it was then, surely, that he would have broken off his irregular liaison, if it in fact existed. The date given by Mrs Crawford, therefore, exactly fits the facts, if that liaison was itself a fact; if it was a figment of hers, the coincidence of dates must have been due to chance, unless she fixed on July-August 1884 with the Rector's death in mind, and that seems most unlikely.

However that may be, there is no doubt that by 1873–4 Mrs Pattison's revulsion from her husband had become insuperable, and that from 1875 or so until her husband's death her interests and affections were concentrated not upon him but upon the man who was to succeed him. One can understand why he began his Diary for 1877 with the words: 'Sad the year opens for me again! My heart is sick from starvation! I have much kindness from many, but love is what I pine for, and have not got.'

Two years later, Pattison found consolation in a new friendship. Six volumes in the Bodleian Library contain the letters that passed between the Rector and Margaret Bradley, niece of the Master of University College, from the end of 1879 until the beginning of 1884.

The Lodgings at Lincoln, while Pattison was Rector, received a succession of young women who sat at his feet, listened to his wisdom, and encouraged him to form their minds. Sometimes a circle would meet for formal 'read-ings', from Browning or a classical author; sometimes instruction was given to a single listener, often a niece of his wife's. Mrs Ward has left us a picture of him on such occasions:

I saw him thus [she wrote] in the winter evenings, when, as a girl, of nineteen, I would sometimes find myself in his library at Lincoln; 'the Rector' on one side of the fire, myself on the other, the cat and the cheerful blaze between. He looked thus as he talked of men and books and University affairs, with a frankness he showed much more readily to women than to men, and to the young rather than to his own contemporaries. He was always interested in the young girl-students of Oxford. He tried to help them, to set a standard before them; and when afterwards that bitter but most impressive fragment of auto-biography appeared—one of the documents of University life in the nineteenth century which no after historian will neglect —there were some of us who read it with no mere intellectual interest, but with a sharp pang at heart that our true friend should have suffered so much and so barrenly.

Half a century later, a niece of his wife's[1] told me of his kindness to her as a girl, affection and pity evidently con-tending in her recollections of 'poor Uncle Mark'; and she left to the Bodleian Library a series of letters in which, between 1879 and 1883, he gave the best of his mind in answer to the questions on life and immortality, 'self-education' and religion, that she poured out to him with the earnestness of youth; 'Whenever you have a good thought', he told her, 'write it down and send it to me without the formalities of an epistle.'

[1] Miss Gertrude Tuckwell (1861–1951), biographer of Sir Charles Dilke; made a C. H. for her services in advancement of women's causes.

That Oxford at the time suspected a sentimental streak in the Rector's interest in his young disciples may be inferred from Walter Pater's unkind remark about the Rector 'romping with great girls among the gooseberry-bushes'; but there seems to be no evidence that confirms the suspicion expressed by that lively image, save in the case of Meta Bradley.

Meta (she was never known by any other name) was getting on for thirty when she entered the Rector's circle; he was more than twice her age. She lived alone, with a deaf father[1] and unsympathetic stepmother in Paddington, devoting herself to social work. She used to come to Oxford to visit her uncle, at University College, and it was on such a visit early in 1879 that she first met the Rector. In a few weeks she had won his confidence and his affection, and in a few months his love.

Just a year after they first met, she described the growth of her own affection:

Do try and imagine yourself a girl who couldn't care very much for her nearest relations [she wrote] and was always being told by them that she had no heart. She didn't agree with them, but was obliged to confess to herself that she didn't like any human being very much—that she never felt any great emotion at the idea of meeting any one or parting from them—in short that she must make up her mind never to see any one for whom she could care deeply and must make no fuss at having to lead a dreary because loveless life. This young woman meets someone of whom she has heard as a man of learning etc. and to her great surprise he actually takes a friendly interest in her. At first she is

[1] Brother of the Rev. Granville Bradley, Headmaster of Marlborough, Master of University College and Dean of Westminster, and half-brother of F. H. and A. C. Bradley.

only grateful and alarmed, but she soon feels that this kind friend somehow feels as lonely and wretched very often as she does and then by degrees she thinks much oftener of him than any one...Can't you imagine, dear Rector, what I feel for the person who has shewn me that I still have a heart?

What he did for her, she in her turn did for him: the 'aged veteran', he told her, 'revived and felt young again—oh how wonderful!—a young heart turning to him with love'. The 'aged veteran' responded: 'I have never yet engaged my heart in any quarter', he wrote, 'without suffering for it...But the die is cast! I have given myself away and am yours.' She rewarded him with complete devotion: 'I don't suppose you will ever understand the sort of feeling which I have for you, a unique mixture of what people feel for their God, their husband and their child.' His affection was less impulsive, but it was real: 'Dearest', he wrote to her, 'as long as I live—though that can't be long—you must remember that you have one friend, all whose thoughts turn towards you and who whatever comes before him involuntarily asks himself what Meta would think of it.'

He did not often express his feelings so openly; it did not come easily to him to do so: 'Though I know I am of a tenderly sympathetic nature', he wrote, early in their correspondence, 'I am aware of a certain chilliness of manner, which keeps me at a distance from those I would most willingly approach.'

Not many months before he died, she complained to him that she was lonely; 'I was quite distressed by your complaint of loneliness', he wrote in reply, 'but on thinking it over I can't see that you are more lonely than the rest of us—those of us I mean who have thought out our destinies. That single fact creates round us a vacuum.' To one who lived in such a vacuum the exchange of affection with another was an unaccustomed luxury: 'I am unable to decide', he wrote, 'which is the greater pleasure, to give or to receive sympathy.' But he did not allow emotion to quench his critical faculty. He would tell Meta that when last he saw her she was looking 'thin, worn, and haggard', and he complained that the narrowness of her social circle had, during the last two years, seriously 'impoverished [her] nature'. Nor was he indulgent towards her trivial misdemeanours: so far from being touched to hear that she had inscribed her name in a book he gave her, he observed 'I do not approve of your writing your name in your great sprawling hand on the fly-leaves of all my books, it is a positive defacement'; and her orthographical deficiencies provoked a satiric comment: 'Why do you always spell across with two c's when everybody else spells it with one? I dare say you are right, but should like to know the reason.'

Undeterred by these severities, she sent him in reply garrulous effusions of gossip and adoration, in the sprawling hand he so much despised.

They wrote regularly, often more than once a week; they met when he visited London, where he stayed at the Athenaeum, using the National Gallery as a rendezvous; the Rector would take her to Lectures or to At Homes, or—one is reminded of the frugality of Professor Forth—to 'lunch at a People's Café'; when Mrs Pattison was abroad Meta came to stay—once, at least, for weeks on end—in his Lodgings at Lincoln. She performed for him one practical service: it was she who urged him to write his reminiscences—'I want to know how the you of Oriel became the you of Lincoln'—and she kept him to the task through many months of illness and depression. He acknowledged the debt by promising that the *Memoirs* should be dedicated to her; 'they are addressed to you', he wrote, 'and no one else'.

This 'strange and perfect friendship', as Meta called it, shocked current notions of propriety, though there is no reason to suppose that they broke the matrimonial law, and of course it stimulated ill-natured Oxford gossip. There was an anonymous letter—the Rector suspected Rhoda Broughton—and Miss Bradley was excluded from certain Oxford drawing-rooms. Mrs Pattison (as he knew) was aware of the situation,[1] resented it, and complained to others (she had her confidants in Oxford and corresponded with them behind his back, referring scathingly to 'the David and Abishag difficulty') but she seems never to have said a word on the subject to her husband.

Six months before he died, further visits by Meta to Oxford became impracticable: his wife insisted on returning from France to look after him. He needed her, but did not want her; she knew this, and it quickened her

---

[1] She (innocently) opened the letter from Meta quoted on p. 49, which reached the Lodgings while he was away from home, and scribbled a message to her husband on a blank page. In his next letter, the Rector warned Meta to be more careful: 'She opens my letters', he told her, 'but would never dream of reading one written by you.'

determination to take her place by his side. He was, though the doctors had not diagnosed it, in the last stages of cancer of the stomach. He urged Meta to marry: 'Marry an old man', he wrote, bidding her live her life and not regret him: 'Be yourself and go bravely on—It is quite silly giving up because an old man of seventy is about to die!'

In June 1884 he was moved to Harrogate, for the waters, but they gave him no relief; and he spent the last six weeks of his life without seeing Meta again or being able to hold communication with her. His wife, who was by his bedside day and night, described in a letter to a friend how she 'asked him if there was any one whom he would like me to ask to stay here'; when he scouted the idea of sisters and nieces, she pressed him: 'Is there *anyone*, I will ask anyone, no matter who, to come.' 'No one you would like', he replied. It was obvious who it was both had in mind, and she must have known that what she suggested was out of the question. Confident that she could exploit her superiority without any risk, she pressed him further: 'My dear soul, that is not what I am thinking of. I want and would like to have *any one* whose presence would be a pleasure to you.' Her victory was now complete: 'You do not know', he replied (if her account is to be trusted), 'what you are yourself—you are all-sufficing. You do not know how good you are to me, you are my comfort and consolation, the only one I want—you are all-sufficing.'

Two days later he died in great agony. The letters written by his wife during his last hours are painful to read: the opiates prescribed by his doctors were not fully effective: 'His screams of pain and terror', she wrote, 'were heard through the house.' 'The moral misery', she added, characteristically, 'is awful. May my last days not be like his.'

Under her husband's will Mrs Pattison took (barring a few small legacies) his whole estate, which amounted to some £50,000; he had inherited money from his mother, and had always been a careful investor. The widow was indignant when she found that by a codicil, which she had known about, but supposed him to have cancelled, Meta, who had hardly anything of her own to live on, had been left a legacy of £5,000; the lawyers advised that it was impossible to invalidate the bequest, and Mrs Pattison, who was also literary executor, contented herself with suppressing the dedication of the *Memoirs* to Meta and concealing the fact by a disingenuous note in the Preface. Perhaps one of the lessons she had learned from her moral mentor George Eliot was how far, in such matters, it is permissible for a really high-minded woman to go.

She vented her bitterness against her husband by forbidding his friends to come to the funeral: 'Many who felt affection and respect for him', said one who knew her well, 'will be sad that they have been prevented from testifying to those feelings by one who felt neither.'

Poor Meta lived on until the 1920s, to be the maiden aunt of many nieces, one of whom was Mrs H. A. L. Fisher. Another of them, Mrs Heseltine, has left a not very kind portrait in her Memoirs of a fussy, rather ridiculous, old lady, about whom lingered rumours of an early indiscretion, 'A romantic infatuation for an elderly and highly distinguished man—whose wife, for reasons of her own, did her best to advertise the affair.'[1]

Unfulfilled and inadequate as it was—for Meta was a pathetic creature without a brain in her head, and quite unworthy of his serious attention—this friendship of his last years seems to have been the only relationship in which Pattison received and bestowed affection without embarrassment. It was the first time in his life that he had found someone who really cared for him and asked nothing from him but to be allowed to worship him. If he appeared to the world to be incapable of feeling deeply for others, that was because he had never mastered the art of expressing his emotions. He recognized this himself. His affection for his sisters, he says in his *Memoirs*, 'was manifested partly in a general rudeness of behaviour towards them, partly in acts of absolute selfishness', adding that he could only wonder that one of them (he meant his sister Fanny) remained devoted to him to the end.

Also there was something in him that made it difficult

[1] *Lost Content* by Olive Heseltine, privately printed, 1948. Meta is also 'Aunt Minnie' in Mrs Heseltine's novel *Three Daughters* (published, under the pseudonym 'Jane Dashwood', in 1930): 'That in some legendary past this aunt had been the victim of a devastating love-affair, had behaved in a manner which Lady Pomfret described as intensely foolish, and caused all her friends and relations the greatest anxiety—even this record could not invest Aunt Minnie's personality with pathos or romance.'

Meta Bradley appears also as Flora Timson ('Tims') in *The Invader*, a novel by her first cousin, Mrs Margaret Woods, a daughter of Dean Bradley; so I have been informed by Mr Gabriel Woods, the authoress's son.

for him to believe that others liked him, or admired him, or wished him well. 'He would pain old and tried friends', said his old pupil James Cotter Morison, 'by expressions of surprise at their attachment. He could not be brought to believe how many loved and regarded him. On one occasion, when I was speaking of the mistakes we are apt to commit in estimating our importance in the world, he answered with his characteristic emphatic "Yes! Take your worst opinion of yourself when you are in most depressed mood. Extract the cube root of that and you will be getting near the common opinion of your merits."' 'There is much that is dreadfully painful', wrote his wife when he was on his deathbed, 'in the persistence of his cruel misconceptions of the conduct of those who have loved him best.'

Those who cannot take love on trust are apt to become unlovable and to be thought themselves unloving. Such a verdict in Pattison's case would have done him less than justice. George Eliot and Rhoda Broughton missed a truth that revealed itself to Mrs Humphry Ward: his affections could be deep and lasting.

You will remember that Newman tells in his *Apologia* how, when he left Oxford in February 1846, Pattison was one of the friends who came to the Radcliffe Observatory to say goodbye to him.

The two men hardly saw each other again. In forty years I can trace only three meetings between them. Once in the 'sixties they met by chance in the train; in 1877 Pattison, lecturing in Birmingham, visited Newman at the

Edgbaston Oratory; in 1878 they met at dinner in Trinity when the Cardinal was in Oxford to celebrate his Honorary Fellowship of his old college.

From time to time, they exchanged letters. In one of these, Pattison, acknowledging a copy of *The Development of Christian Doctrine*, reminded its author that thirty-two years had elapsed since he placed on his shelves a copy of the first edition of the book. 'Thirty-two years!', he exclaims, 'I cannot trust myself to speak of the many threads which connect heart and mind with that distant time. Another and yet the same! I often wonder if other men have gone through such a mental change without losing their personal identity.'

It was in his attitude towards Christianity and the Catholic Church that Pattison had changed most completely. He who had once been on the brink of Rome, summed up his final judgement on the Christian religion in a letter he wrote towards the end of his life, in which he spoke of the 'infinitesimally small effect produced by the intervention of the Almighty 1900 years ago. As I saw it put some where [he said]: The Devil has (on the Christian scheme) far the best of the struggle, and that without killing his only Son.'

Still, he did not advertise his religious scepticism or allow it to affect his everyday life. To renounce Holy Orders would have been ridiculous; besides, it would have meant giving up his position and its emoluments—a crippling sacrifice that would have served no useful purpose. So he continued to the end of his days to officiate, and to administer the sacrament, in the college chapel.

None the less, he was aggressively anti-clerical and anti-ecclesiastical in speech and writing. His letters abound in scathing reference to 'idiotic parsons' and 'round-collared boobies'; 'I doubt very much the truth of the proposition that priests believe in the Gods they worship', he wrote to Gertrude Tuckwell; 'Prophets are fanatical, and believe; but priests are generally professional quacks trading in beliefs they do not share.' This bitterness affected his historical judgements. Dean Church put it well in a review of the posthumous *Essays*: Pattison, he said,

had passed from the extreme ranks and strong convictions of the Oxford movement...to the frankest form of Liberal thought. As he himself writes, we cannot give up early beliefs, much less the deep and deliberate convictions of manhood, without some shock to the character. In his case the change certainly worked. It made him hate what he had left, and all that was like it, with the bitterness of one who had been imposed upon, and has been led to commit himself to what he now feels to be absurd and contemptible, and the bitterness of this disappointment gave an edge to all his work.

During his last illness a letter reached him from the man who had distorted his life by leading him to the brink from which he recoiled with such violence and disgust. I will quote it in full:

The Oratory, Birmingham: Dec. 27, 1883

My very dear Pattison,—I grieve to hear that you are very unwell. How is it that I, who am so old, am carried on in years beyond my juniors?

This makes me look back in my thoughts forty years, when you, with Dalgairns and so many others now gone, were entering into life.

For the sake of those dear old days, I cannot help writing to you. Is there any way in which I can serve you? At least I can give you my prayers, such as they are.

Yours affectionately,

JOHN H. CARD. NEWMAN

Pattison suspected that this letter was prompted partly by the desire to save his soul by converting him at the last moment to the Church of Rome; and in this he was right, as Newman's subsequently published correspondence shows. It is not difficult to see the Rector perusing this letter with a thin-lipped, cynical, smile; and, when one thinks of the bitter comments it might well have evoked from him, one's instinctive feeling is a hope that he left it unanswered.

In fact, he answered it as follows:

Lincoln College, Oxford: Dec. 28, 1883

When your letter, my dear master, was brought to my bedside this morning and I saw your well-known handwriting, my eyes filled so with tears that I could not at first see to read what you had said.

When I found in what affectionate terms you addressed me, I felt guilty, for I thought, would he do so, if he knew how far I have travelled on the path which leads quite away from those ideas which I once—about 1845–1846—shared with him?

Or is your toleration so large, that though you knew me to be in grievous error, you could still embrace me as a son?

If I have not dared to approach you in any way of recent years, it has been only from the fear that you might be regarding me as coming to you under false colours.

The veneration and affection which I felt for you at the time you left us, are in no way diminished, and however remote my intellectual standpoint may now be from that which I may presume to be your own, I can still truly say that I have learnt more from you than from any one else with whom I have ever been in contact.

Let me subscribe myself for the last time

Your affectionate son and pupil,

MARK PATTISON

Here is Newman's brief reply:

January 2, 1884

My dear Pattison,—On consideration I find it a duty to answer your question to me about toleration.

I am then obliged to say that what Catholics hold upon it, I hold with them.

That God, who knows the heart, may bless you now and ever is the fervent prayer of your most affectionate friend

JOHN H. CARD. NEWMAN

It was winter, and the Cardinal was over eighty, and he had hardly recovered from a recent attack of bronchitis; but, a few days later, he took the train to Oxford from Snow Hill. Pattison's niece, who was then a girl of twenty and acting as his house-keeper, gave me some years ago her recollections of the visit. The two men spent an hour or so alone together, and Pattison, in one of his last letters to Meta Bradley, described what passed between them. It is enough to say that their conversation was governed by the spirit of the letters I have quoted.

If Newman and Pattison were antithetical figures in the Oxford of their day, so also, in a different way, were Pattison and Jowett. They were a pair of opposites, but they were always a pair. Mrs Ward has described them, at the tail of the procession in St Mary's: 'the long line of Heads of Houses, in their scarlet robes as Doctors of Divinity, all but the two heretics, Pattison and Jowett, who always walked in their plain black'. Pattison despised Jowett's scholarship; and Jowett must have known it. But when, in the autumn of 1884, there fell to Jowett, as Vice-Chancellor, the duty of paying tribute to those whom the University had lost during the preceding year, he delivered a long and generous account of the Rector, in the course of which he used these surprising by perceptive words:

Qui si paullo tristior ac severior nonnullis esse videretur ego potius ita censeo, neminem unquam humaniorem fuisse hoc homine, qui de caritate et benevolentia suorum tamquam omnis penderet.

To some he may have seemed rather too austere in his own life and too harsh in the judgements that he passed on others. It is my opinion, on the contrary, that there never was a more truly human being than he, and he would have been lost without the love and kindly feeling of those who were close to him.

3

PATTISON'S OXFORD

Mark Pattison was destined for Oxford from the day of his birth. He tells us so himself. 'There never was any question as to my destination', he wrote. 'It was assumed, from the cradle upwards, that I was to go to Oxford, and to be a Fellow of a College.' For this future he was trained at his father's knee. Like many eminent Victorians—like Newman, and Ruskin, and Carlyle, and Browning, and Tennyson, and Dickens, and Mill, and Disraeli—he was not the product of a public school. He was prepared for the University by his father at Hauxwell Rectory, with no outside assistance except a couple of months' tuition in mathematics from a Cambridge graduate.

However much he lost through going without a regular school-education, there was one thing that he gained: his sensibility was never coated with the varnish imparted by schoolmasters or padded with the protective covering developed by contact with schoolfellows; he went up to Oxford capable of receiving a vivid impression from his new surroundings; he was a freshman who could truly be described as 'raw'. He was, he said himself, a sort of Caspar Hauser; it was at Oxford that he made his first contact with his kind.

He reached Oriel in 1832 with high expectations. He fondly supposed that he was entering 'an honourable company of rivalry in the pursuit of knowledge'. Oriel, together with Balliol, had the reputation of being one of the two colleges where studious interests were not only not frowned upon but positively encouraged, and he hoped to find intellectual companions among his fellow-students. He was bitterly disappointed: 'I found lectures regarded as a joke or a bore, contemned by the more advanced, shirked by the backward; Latin and Greek regarded as useless, except for the purpose of getting a degree.' In his innocence, he was surprised by this: it seemed to him, he said, looking back later, 'a paradox...that men should come to a University not to study'.[1]

It was certainly in order to study that he himself went up to Oxford. He tells us in his *Memoirs* that his father was fond of repeating a sentence from the Eton Latin Grammar: *Concessi Cantabrigiam ad capiendum ingenii cultum*—'I withdrew to Cambridge to improve my mind'. This, he says, 'was the proverb which presided over my whole life... I think no other sentence of any book had so large a share in moulding my mind and character as that one.' *Ingenii cultus*, mental culture, the improvement of his mind; it is the literal truth that that remained to its end the dominating purpose of his life.

[1] To his companions, he himself seemed an equally strange figure. 'We used to call him *Philosopher Pat*', wrote one of them, years afterwards; 'His temperament was cold, including even his bodily nature. After a brisk walk to the top of Headington Hill, when other men would have been all aglow with exercise, his hands were as clammy as though he had not walked a hundred yards. His thin close-set lips would be silent for a time, and then he would come out with something worth discussing, on which his inner consciousness seemed to have been feeding. He was keenly sarcastic, whether Politics, Theology, or Oxford Life were the subject.'

If he was disappointed in the undergraduates of Oxford, Pattison was even more deeply disillusioned by the dons. He had looked to them to be his leaders and guides on entering the promised land of intellect that he supposed was awaiting him at Oriel. Here again, his hopes were not fulfilled.

Gibbon said that he reached Oxford with 'a stock of education, that might have puzzled a doctor, and a degree of ignorance, of which a schoolboy would have been ashamed'. Pattison when he went up to Oriel was both less learned and less ignorant. He was familiar with a fair range of the easier Greek and Latin authors; but he had simply read the texts with the help of a lexicon, his father correcting him out of a crib; he had no idea, he tells us, of the niceties of scholarship, or of the literary quality of what he read. He had, in fact, no more than a smattering of classical knowledge; but even this was enough to put him not only ahead of his fellow-undergraduates, but on a level with his tutors. His first 'lecture' was a class on the *Alcestis*:

When we came to the first lyrics, Φοῖβ' ἀδικεῖς αὖ τιμὰς ἐνέρων, etc., the tutor put the question, 'What metre is this?' It went the round, no one had any idea; it came to me, and I remember the trembling excitement with which I answered, 'Anapaestic dimeter'... Monk had a note on the metre of the passage, and most of the class had Monk, but they had not read the Latin note. Denison gave me a look as much as to say, 'Who the devil are you?' He had evidently not been accustomed in his class to meet with such profound learning. I do not remember in the whole course of the term that Denison made a single remark on the two plays, *Alcestis* and *Hippolytus*, that did not come from Monk's notes.

'In less than a week', he declares, 'I was entirely disillusioned as to what I was to learn in an Oxford lecture-room.'

'An Oxford lecture-room' meant something quite different in 1832 from what it means today. First of all, lecturing was a college affair: lectures were given by college tutors, in college to members of their own college only. The tutor never lectured to an outside audience; the pupil depended, so far as official instruction went, on the lectures of his own college. There were, indeed, a score or so of Professors, but they were not required to lecture often, and most of them lectured less often than they were required to. I see from the University Calendar for 1832 that the occupant of the newly founded Chair of Political Economy held his appointment jointly with the Archbishopric of Dublin. Even a conscientious professor often found it hard to collect an audience; in the same year, 1832, Baden Powell, Savilian Professor of Geometry, opened a lecture with the words: 'In my Courses of Public Lectures (whenever, namely, by the circumstances of a class being collected, I have been able to give any)'—and he went on to complain that he found it almost impossible to procure an audience because the study of Mathematics was not given its proper place in the curriculum of the University. This was true of most of the subjects for which professorial chairs existed (e.g. Law, Medicine, Hebrew, Anglo-Saxon, Modern History, Astronomy, Music, Poetry): they lay outside the course of the Schools, which consisted of the rudiments of Religion (the Gospels in Greek, Old and New Testament history; the XXXIX Articles, and Paley's *Evidences*), Literae Humaniores (the Greek and Latin languages and Ancient History, and Rhetoric and Poetry and Moral and Political Philosophy, as taught by classical writers), and the elements of Mathematics and Physics.[1]

For practical purposes, therefore, professorial lectures were irrelevant, and since undergraduates were not admitted to lectures in colleges other than their own, they depended for official instruction entirely on the tutors of their own colleges.

In each college, two (or, in the larger colleges, three) tutors undertook all the teaching, usually with the help of an assistant-lecturer in mathematics. Sometimes the tutors divided the subjects between themselves, sometimes they divided the pupils, which meant that each tutor had to be prepared to teach every subject—'In some colleges', said W. C. Lake of Balliol (referring to 1950, when the curriculum had been extended), 'the same Tutor lectures on seven or eight or more subjects at once.'

This system might have been adequate if the tutors generally had been keen and well-qualified teachers. But college tutors were neither. They were chosen from among the Fellows, and the Fellows were elected without any

[1] In 1839 a Statute making attendance at certain professorial lectures a pre-requisite for a Degree was introduced by the Hebdomadal Board; it was thrown out by Congregation, the majority evidently regarding such a requirement as a criticism of, and a threat to, the tutorial system.

Among the correspondence at Apsley House is a letter from the Vice-Chancellor reporting on the matter to the Duke as Chancellor; in the past, said the Vice-Chancellor, attendance at professors' lectures had been compulsory, but 'as the subjects which the Professors have to lecture on have become obsolete', the need to attend them was gradually dispensed with and in fact the lectures were not delivered.

regard to their tutorial qualifications. In fact, being a tutor was not well enough paid to be looked upon as a vocation or a profession or even a regular post; a tutorship was simply a perquisite, a job with which a junior Fellow could occupy a year or two while he was waiting for a college living. When a tutorship became vacant, the Head of the College would offer the post to the Fellows in residence in order of seniority, without regard to their abilities, usually passing over those who were not in Orders.

Of course the result was that most tutors were, in both senses of the word, indifferent teachers; many of them thought they had done all that was required of them if they could keep just ahead of their pupils. A reasonably diligent college tutor might have managed to do this under the system that ruled in the eighteenth century, when under-graduates were neither expected nor, usually, encouraged to work; when there were no Honours Schools to read for; and when the examination for degrees was a formality that had degenerated into a farce. But by the time Pattison came into residence very different conditions prevailed.

It is often said that Oxford did not emerge from the eighteenth century until half way through the nineteenth. Broadly speaking, that is true. It is true of the constitution of the University in both its senses, the composition of the academic body and its machinery of government: the way in which the colleges recruited their fellows and their undergraduates remained practically unaltered from the seventeenth century until the passage of the great reforming

Act of 1854; so did the system of academic government, the oligarchy exercised by the Hebdomadal Board consisting of the Heads of Houses. But in the curriculum and in the method of examination for degrees, reform had started half a century earlier.

The old system had become a notorious scandal. 'At the beginning of this century', said Newman, 'matters were at the worst at Oxford. The degrees were at that time taken upon no *bona fide* examination. The youth, who had passed his three or four years at the place, and wished to graduate, chose his examiners, and invited them to dinner, which the ceremony of the examination preceded.' And the 'ceremony' was indeed no more than a ceremony, the examiners asking questions that were entirely frivolous or enabled the candidate to rehearse answers that he had learned by heart. The process, as it existed in 1780, is described by Vicesimus Knox:

Every candidate is obliged to be examined in the whole circle of the sciences by three Masters of Arts, of his own choice. The examination is to be holden in one of the public schools, and to continue from nine o'clock till eleven. The Masters take a most solemn oath that they will examine properly and impartially. Dreadful as all this appears, there is always found to be more of appearance in it than reality, for the greatest dunce usually gets his testimonium signed with as much ease and credit as the finest genius. The manner of proceeding is as follows: The poor young man to be examined in the sciences often knows no more of them than his bedmaker, and the Masters who examine are sometimes equally unacquainted with such mysteries. But schemes, as they are called, or little books, containing 40 or 50 questions in each science, are handed down from age to age, from one to another. The Candidate to be examined employs three or four days in learning these by heart, and the Examiners, having done the same before him when they were examined, know what questions to ask, and so all goes on smoothly. When the Candidate has displayed his universal knowledge of the sciences, he is to display his skill in Philology. One of the Masters, therefore, desires him to construe a passage in some Greek or Latin classic, which he does with no interruption, just as he pleases, and as well as he can. The Statutes next require that he should translate familiar English phrases into Latin. And now is the time when the Masters show their wit and jocularity. Droll questions are put on any subject, and the puzzled Candidate furnishes diversion in his awkward embarrassment. I have known the questions on this occasion to consist of an inquiry into the pedigree of a race-horse.

The first step towards turning this ceremony into a real examination had been taken as long ago as the first year of the century. This was the Examination Statute of 1800, which was passed at the instance of three great Heads of Houses, Cyril Jackson, Dean of Christ Church, John Eveleigh, Provost of Oriel, and John Parsons, Master of Balliol. The new Examination Statute marked an epoch in the history of Oxford studies. It instituted, for all candidates for the B.A. degree, a compulsory examination that was a real examination and not a mere formality. The candidates were to be examined in certain Greek and Latin books, chosen by them from an extensive list, and in the elements of logic and mathematics: the examiners were appointed by the proctors and paid by the University; the examination was conducted in public.

The Examination Statute made another, even more important, change: it instituted a special, voluntary, examination in the same subjects, which could be taken instead of the ordinary examination by those who wanted to prove their superior abilities; and it provided that the examiners should publish, in order of merit, the names of the candidates who deserved special distinction. This was the beginning of the system of Honours Degrees that has, for better or worse, continued in Oxford ever since.

In 1807, two further changes were introduced. The first change broadened the curriculum: side by side with Literae Humaniores, the examination in Greek and Latin and logic, there was established an examination in elementary mathematics and physics; all candidates for the B.A. degree had to pass in both these examinations and could compete for Honours in either or both of them. The second change was the introduction of a formal system of classes: the names of those awarded Honours in each examination were to be placed in two classes, the names in each class in alphabetical order. So for the first time it was possible for a versatile student to obtain a double first, by being placed in the first class in each of the two Final Schools, Literae Humaniores and mathematics and physics.[1]

During the first thirty years of the century there followed a series of Statutes that further modernized both the procedure in the examination and the field it covered. Hitherto, the proceedings had been entirely oral, a method so cumbrous that in 1822 it took the examiners twelve weeks to get through the two hundred candidates

---

[1] The first man to achieve this distinction was Sir Robert Peel, who took his degree in 1808; the next was John Keble, who was one of two candidates with a Double First in 1810.

who presented themselves: now, written papers were introduced. Also, the results were presented differently: a line drawn below the names of the superior candidates divided the second class into two (1809); those below the line were, presently, allotted to a separate third class (1825); finally, in 1830, a fourth class was added.

Then the field covered by Literae Humaniores was extended so that instead of being purely literary and philological it included ancient history and moral and political philosophy; later, in 1850, further (optional) Schools were added, in natural science, in law and modern history (at first combined, then split into two separate Schools), and (in 1870) theology. All candidates for the B.A. degree had to pass in Lit. Hum. and in one or other, at their option, of the other Schools.[1]

By the time Pattison came up to Oriel in 1832, this Honours system had thoroughly established itself; it was reckoned that 30 per cent of the undergraduates read for a Class and not a Pass. The system under which a college tutor undertook to teach all subjects was plainly inadequate, now that undergraduate studies covered a wide range and led to a formidable examination, which was taken seriously by the undergraduates themselves. And this inadequacy gave rise to a recognized anomaly in the

[1] To complete the story: in 1850 'Honour Moderations' was interposed between Responsions and the final School in Lit. Hum., thus creating the *cursus* of 'Mods' and 'Greats' that still continues; it was not until 1874 that Lit. Hum. was deprived of its supremacy by being made an alternative to the other Final Schools instead of being compulsory for all candidates. Greek remained a compulsory element in Responsions, the initial elementary examination, until the early 1920s, as Latin is still for those who do not take Science.

Oxford teaching system: it became the accepted practice for the man who hoped for Honours to supplement college tuition, or to supply its place, by going to a private tutor or 'coach'. The private tutor was usually a young B.A.; he was not always a Fellow of a college, though he might be; he might even be a Fellow of the same college as the pupil; in any event, the pupil's arrangement with him was an entirely private one.

Every undergraduate, therefore, paid his college a tuition fee, in return for which he was so inadequately instructed that, if he took his work at all seriously, he had to pay a further fee[1] to obtain from a private coach the help that his college tutor ought to have given him. It is an odd paradox that the personal relationship between tutor and pupil, developed in the individual 'tutorial hour', which is supposed to give Oxford and Cambridge so great an advantage over other Universities today, should have its archetype (in Oxford, at any rate) in the relation between the pupil and his private coach, which was no part of the university system, but an excrescence that came into being as a result of its defects, like a plant that had sown itself on a decaying college wall.

Pattison as an undergraduate was a victim of this inadequate system of tuition. The year before he came up, three exceptional Oriel tutors, John Henry Newman, Richard Hurrell Froude, and Robert Wilberforce, any one of whom might have given him the help and

[1] The regular fee for coaching seems to have been £10 a term for an hour every other day, £20 a term for an hour a day.

encouragement he was looking for, had been dismissed by the Provost, Hawkins, and three incompetent nonentities appointed in their place.

Pattison needed no help to pass Responsions at the end of his first year; it was an examination so elementary that he could have passed it without any assistance as soon as he came up; but when he came to Literae Humaniores he was at a loss: 'For want of guidance', he said, 'I was wholly at sea.' He went to the College lecture-course on Aristotle's *Rhetoric*: 'But such a lecture!—the tutor incapable of explaining any difficulty, and barely able to translate the Greek, even with the aid of a crib.'

Our misfortunes are sometimes blessings in disguise, and our greatest successes are sometimes due to our own deficiences: his College's failure to supply him with what he needed, and the parsimonious streak that prevented him from putting himself immediately in the hands of a private coach, determined Pattison's whole mental history. Instead of spending the next, formative, years being coached by a tutor with his eyes fixed on an examination, he attacked the fortress of learning single-handed. In his diary, that Long Vacation, he entered his resolve: 'To improve and enlarge my mind by every means.' *Cantabrigiam concessi ad capiendum ingenii cultum*—if the University could not improve his mind for him, he would improve it for himself. He sat down and laid out a programme of reading. His programme bore no relation to what he needed for the Schools; it covered the whole field of classical literature, of philosophy, of history. When he looked back on this programme in after-life, he said that it had only one fault: it needed years for its realization. 'I may say that I have been all my life occupied in carrying out and developing the ideal that I conceived in July, 1833, more than 50 years ago.'

His case was like Gibbon's, at Magdalen, eighty years before: if Gibbon had been properly looked after and instructed by his tutors, we might never have had the *Decline and Fall*. And, as it happened, Gibbon's *Autobiography* fell into Pattison's hands just at that time, and provided him with an example and an inspiration: 'The minute history of a self-education conducted on so superb a scale, was just what I wanted...Gibbon, in fact, supplied the place of a College tutor; he not only found me advice, but secretly inspired me with the enthusiasm to follow it.'

So he pursued a lonely course of self-education, at the expense of the work that was needed if he was to get a First Class in the Schools. As the date of the examination drew near, he panicked, and had recourse to private tuition; he went first to one coach, then changed him for another; postponed his entry for the examination by six months, till the Spring of 1836; and, when the results were announced, was relieved to learn that he had got nothing worse than a Second Class.

It looked like a fatal blow to his hopes of a life devoted to study in the University. But he did not allow the blow to knock him out; his father paid for him to stay on in Oxford, and he settled down to continue his reading in the hope of getting a fellowship.

During the next two years he competed four times for a

fellowship at different colleges, each time unsuccessfully, and he had almost abandoned hope and resigned himself to spending the rest of his life buried in a country parsonage, when in 1839 another chance of a fellowship presented itself. It was at Lincoln, a college with which he had no associations; but he was qualified for the fellowship by his Yorkshire birth; he went in for it, and was elected. He never forgot that November morning in 1839 'when Radford's servant came in to announce my election and to claim his five shillings for doing so'. 'No moment in all my life', he wrote in his *Memoirs*, 'has ever been so sweet.'

So Pattison's career in the University entered on its second phase: he was to experience the tutorial system no longer as an undergraduate, but as a tutor. The ten years that followed were the happiest and most successful of his life. They were the years on which he looked back with most and with least satisfaction. With least satisfaction, because during this period he was sucked, as he put it, into the whirlpool of Tractarianism. The process had already begun when he was elected in 1839. If the Fellows of Lincoln had known how far he had already gone along the path to Rome they would never have elected him to a fellowship. Twenty years later, in 1861, they would never have elected him to the Rectorship if they had known how completely he had lost his faith.

From 1840 to 1842, he says, he was 'consumed by a fury of zeal'; his reason 'seemed entirely in abeyance'. He 'once got so low by fostering a morbid state of conscience as to go to confession to Dr Pusey'. 'Years afterwards', he adds—and I have no doubt that he believed it, but see no reason why we should—'it came to my knowledge that Pusey had told a fact about myself, which he got from me on that occasion, to a friend of his, who employed it to annoy me.'

It became a legend in Oxford that if he had not missed the coach to Birmingham Pattison would have followed Newman when (as he put it) 'the crash came' in 1845. He says himself, and his unpublished correspondence confirms it, that he was hovering on the brink in those years and that he was saved mainly by being appointed a college tutor in 1843.[1] This meant hard and absorbing work, and it also gave him an immediate object: he set himself to be a first-rate tutor, and he succeeded. 'I never', he says, 'could let routine be routine, or do anything with any comfort to myself, unless I tried to do it as well as I could.' Sometimes he would give four hour-long lectures in a single morning. He 'invented' a lecture on Aristotle that gave him more trouble, he said, than anything he ever undertook. In vacation he took his pupils on reading-parties; he tried to interest them in poetry, in literature, in the things of the mind. This is how an old pupil describes his methods:

Mr Pattison was not a successful maker of 'first classes'. He did not give to his pupils ready-made conclusions in mental science or history which might be conveniently reproduced in exami-

[1] Looking back on those days, Pusey himself said that Pattison 'started back from the very threshold of Rome. His mind was one which could only see consistency in extremes. Since he could not become Roman he became what he has become. We expected him to become a Roman Catholic the earliest of all' (J. B. Atlay, *Memoir of Sir H. W. Acland*, 1903, pp. 415–16).

nations. It was his chief complaint against the 'Final Classical Schools' at Oxford that they tended to produce in teachers and taught the habit of constructing and appropriating such conclusions. He used to send us away from his lectures with the feeling of roused inquiry, rather than with that satisfied sense of acquisition which is so conducive to success. But he made us think. He made us desire to know. He taught us to enter into the real minds of Aristotle and Plato, rather than to furnish ourselves with well-formulated theories of what they wrote.[1]

And it was not only the reading men among his pupils that felt his influence, nor only in the lecture-room that he exerted it; here is a rowing man, turned country parson, writing to his old tutor ten years after he had taken his degree:

Neither the old love nor the old *statu pupillari* reverence in me have ever drooped for a single moment... You were the first who held out a hand to raise me from the slough-of-despond of an extreme (at least intellectual) self-depreciation. You were the man—the very Angel of God—who led me back, by leading strings I could neither see nor feel, to the ways of reason and freedom, just as I was blundering on the brink of spiritual suicide.

By 1850 he could say that he 'wielded almost absolute authority' in Lincoln; he had 'invested his whole heart and pride in it', and he had brought it into the front rank of Oxford colleges.

One has to read between the lines of the *Memoirs* to understand what it was in him that enabled him to do this; his good qualities are suppressed by a habit of self-depreciation that became a second nature. But he confesses that he

[1] A. J. Church, *Spectator*, 2 Aug. 1884; see also his *Memories* (1908).

had a gift that was 'very slowly making itself felt' during these years: 'In dealing with the students', he says, 'I soon became aware that I was the possessor of a magnetic influence, which...gave me a moral ascendency in the College, to which at last everybody, the Rector, even the students, the very servants...succumbed.'

He had not the sweet and affectionate nature and the instinctive perception of their spiritual needs that cast a spell over Newman's pupils, nor that mixture of innocence and shrewdness, of worldliness and moral purpose, that made Jowett so successful as an adviser of the young. Pattison did not charm his pupils or humour them; but he made them feel that he lived for learning and for them. Let me quote A. J. Church once more:

For the feeling with which Mr Pattison was regarded by the more serious undergraduates, I can find no more appropriate term than reverence. He was not popular in the ordinary sense of the word. *That*, a manner, for the most part, cold and constrained, forbade. Who that ever underwent the awful experience could forget those speechless interviews, when, as etiquette demanded, we reported ourselves at the beginning of term to the Sub-Rector (as he then was), and sate shrinking under what seemed the stony glare that came from over his spectacles? At the same time, he was not unpopular. His severity—and he could be severe on occasion—never gave offence... Those who understood him least, and least felt his influence, had a vague awe of his learning and power. With the more thoughtful there were no limits to the veneration felt for him.

If he was austere, he was not dull; if he was learned, he was not merely bookish; if he was earnest, he was not solemn. He had a dry humour and a sharp wit. When he

was told the undergraduate verses mocking Jowett's
assumption of omniscience:

> Here am I, my name is Jowett
> There's no knowledge but I know it
> What I don't know isn't knowledge,
> I am Master of this College—

Pattison observed 'How clever the young men are now-
days! They discover at once what it has taken us years to
find out.'

But if he impressed the undergraduates of his college, he
was not so popular with his colleagues in the Senior
Common Room. Mr V. H. H. Green, the present
Chaplain of Lincoln, has published, in *Oxford Common
Room*, an excellent picture of the College during the
nineteenth century. It was a small society, with only a
dozen fellows; and it was, unlike Oriel, an obscure college.
It was also a backward and reactionary college. The fellows,
according to Pattison, 'were a bad lot, the tradition of 1750
surviving into the 19th century'. Pattison had a sharp
tongue, and never concealed his scorn for those he con-
sidered his inferiors: 'Queen's and Magdalen, Jesus and
St John's', he said, 'were bad enough, but none of them
could show such fossil specimens of the genus Fellow as our
Kay *senior*, Thompson, Calcott, Meredith.' His general
opinion of his colleagues may be gathered from his
observation after a meeting to elect a butler for the
Common Room; 'The taste of the Fellows for the inferior in everything', he wrote, 'asserted itself, and they
chose the most inferior man they could find—a goggle-
eyed baboon who can't speak English.'

He put them to shame by his earnestness, his passion for mental culture and moral improvement, his diligence as a tutor. The dinner-hour in Lincoln was five o'clock; Pattison would regularly leave the Common Room at eight, to spend two tutorial hours with his pupils, leaving his colleagues and their guests to bet each other bottles of port about the value of the next living to fall vacant, or the names of the last twenty winners of the Derby.

Nor was he content to be different from his colleagues, to let them go their way while he went his own. He was an incorrigible reformer. He could not see anything being done without asking himself whether it could be done better. 'I cannot travel by railway without working out in my mind a better time-table than that in use.' And if he thought an improvement was practicable, he was not happy until it had actually been effected. This applied both to what others did and to what he did himself. Of course this meant upsetting existing arrangements; Pattison did not mind that. It also meant upsetting people who were attached to those arrangements; he did not mind that either. 'There never was anyone', he said, 'to whom it was more impossible not to be a liberal than it was to me'—and for 'liberal' he might have written 'radical'.

At this time, reform was in the air in Oxford. For the dozen years preceding the secession of Newman in 1845 the Tractarian Movement had distracted the minds of all Oxford men with questions of religious doctrine and ecclesiastical allegiance. Then, when Newman 'went', the University woke up like a man who has overslept, when the shutters are removed and the mid-day sun streams in. For the next decade Oxford was flooded with pamphlets of a different kind—no longer about the Tracts, or Baptismal Regeneration, or the Development of Doctrine, or the XXXIX Articles, but about the examination system, the professoriate, the claims of natural science, the restrictions on fellowships, the necessity of altering the college statutes, of reforming the government of the University. The rebels of the day were no longer ecclesiastical apostates, like W. G. Ward; they were political and academic radicals like Goldwin Smith, Disraeli's 'wild man of the Cloister'.

Pattison said that if any Oxford man had gone to sleep in 1846 and woken up in 1850, he would have found himself in a totally new world.

In 1846 we were in Old Tory Oxford: not somnolent because it was as fiercely debating, as in the days of Henry VIII, its eternal Church question. There were Tory majorities in all the colleges; there was the unquestioning satisfaction in the tutorial system, i.e. one man teaching everybody everything; the same belief that all knowledge was shut up between the covers of four Greek and four Latin books; the same humdrum questions asked in the examination; and the same arts of evasive reply. In 1850 all this was suddenly changed as if by the wand of a magician.

A restless fever of change had spread through the colleges— the wonder-working phrase, University reform, had been uttered, and that in the House of Commons. The sounds seemed to breathe new life into us. We against reform! Why, it was the very thing we had been so long sighing for; we were ready to reform a great deal—everything—only show us how to set about it and give us the necessary powers.

But to make the change was not easy, because the existing system was deeply entrenched.

Let me try and give you a picture, painted with a few broad strokes, of the University in the late 1840s.

First, it was about one-fifth of its present size. There were rather more than 500 fellows and about 1,400 undergraduates; these, together with just over twenty heads of colleges and halls—nineteen colleges and four or five halls of residence—and a score or so of professors (a few of whom were fellows) and perhaps a dozen university officers, made up the total academic population.

Only about one-third of the five hundred fellows lived in Oxford; of those who did reside, most were college officers—bursars, tutors, or chaplains. Fellowships were tenable for life, but were forfeited if the fellow married or took a college living or a living of above a certain annual value. Fellowships were worth from £200 to £500 a year (the Commission of 1850 suggested that they should be fixed at £300); even allowing for the changed value of money, this was not enough—had marriage been permitted—to marry on with comfort. And there was no academical ladder to be climbed in Oxford; a fellowship led to no office in the University; it was regarded simply as a prize, which helped you on while you were waiting for a living or in your early professional years—say, at the Bar—if you were not in Orders. When you were earning enough to make marriage possible, or when the expected living dropped, you resigned your fellowship and took a wife.

Oxford in the mid-nineteenth century was an entirely Anglican and largely clerical society: it contained no Dissenters, no Roman Catholics and, among the dons, a minority of laymen. Every undergraduate had to sign a declaration that he had read the XXXIX Articles, and to subscribe to them in order to qualify for a degree. Most fellowships required their holders to take Holy Orders, and for many undergraduates the degree was simply a step on the road to ordination; it has been calculated that of rather over 25,000 men who matriculated at Oxford in the first half of the century, about 1,400 were called to the Bar, and over 10,000 were ordained; Oxford, in other words, was turning out about 200 clergymen a year.

All fellows resident in Oxford of course lived in College; all undergraduates lived in College or in a hall of residence; there was no North Oxford for dons, there were no lodgings for undergraduates.

This collection of small self-contained collegiate communities, composed of fewer than 2,000 men, *was* Oxford. The University, as distinct from the colleges, scarcely existed. There were, in effect, no university institutions apart from the Bodleian Library, the University Church, the University Press, the old Ashmolean Museum. There were only a handful of professors, who played, as we have seen, little part in the business of instructing undergraduates. There were no Faculties; there was no 'Science Area'; the University provided one room in the Clarendon Building for the professors to lecture in. There were, incidentally, no inter-university games except cricket (the first match against Cambridge was played in 1827)—there was not even, until 1829, a university boat-race.

The disparity between the importance of the University and that of the colleges reflected, or at least coincided with, a disparity in wealth: the colleges were rich, while the University was desperately poor; the annual revenues of the University amounted to about £30,000, those of the colleges to several hundreds of thousands of pounds a year, with a further £15,000 p.a. arising from special Trust Funds. Christ Church and Magdalen had each of them an income that by itself exceeded that of the University— spent, in the case of Magdalen, on forty fellows and as many scholars (called 'demies').

As for the government of Oxford, that was in the hands of a despotic Council of Ten—or, rather, of Twenty— the Vice-Chancellor and Proctors and the Heads of Houses, called the Hebdomadal Board because they met once a week. The Heads were invariably in Orders, they were allowed to marry, and they were of course appointed for life. So they formed, both socially and in their outlook, a tiny, closed, and isolated community—a microcosm within a microcosm. Something of the aura that sur-rounded them may be gathered from the description of a contemporary observer, who speaks of 'The heads of houses, in dignified connubial life, within the precincts of which few, except of their own status, were invited to enter, and from which they only seemed to emerge, pre-ceded by the dignified mace-bearers, to take their places in the College chapels, at University sermons, or the aca-demical deliberations in the Convocation House'. Plainly, their age, their status, and their outlook cut them off not only from the undergraduate body but from the fellows of colleges other than their own.[1]

Such an inward-looking body was clearly 'unfit to be the motive power in the place'. But there was no other 'motive power'. The two general assemblies of the University, Congregation (which consisted of all resident graduates) and Convocation (which comprised all graduates with their names on college books) were virtually powerless. The proceedings of Congregation were entirely formal, and though Convocation could, it is true, approve or reject measures proposed by the Hebdomadal Board, it could not itself initiate legislation; and since it had no power of amending measures proposed by the Board, and since its debates had to be conducted in Latin,[2] its sole function in practice was to act as a sort of long-stop: in the unlikely event of the Hebdomadal Board's proposing a reform disagreeable to the conservatively minded, there always remained the hope that Convocation could summon up to Oxford enough of the country clergy to see that it was thrown out.

The whole of the university structure, then, was built upon the college fellowships: the ruling body was the Board of the heads of colleges, who were chosen by the

[1] I am told that when fellows were allowed to retain their fellowships after marriage, so that the don's wife became a recognized branch of the human species, a separate entrance was reserved at Elliston and Cavell's, the Selfridge's of Oxford, for the wives of Heads of Houses.

[2] 'It is a strange solecism', observed one of those who submitted evidence to the Commission of 1850, 'to conduct the business of the nineteenth century in the language of the first.'

fellows; the instruction of the undergraduates was in the hands of the fellows; the life of the University was lived in the colleges, which were run by the fellows; the wealth of the place belonged to the colleges and was spent upon their fabric—chapels, libraries, kitchens and cellars— and it was between the fellows, resident and non-resident alike, that the surplus was divided.

So it was upon the quality and character of the fellows that the quality and character of the University depended; they were, in effect, the trustees of an important national trust. It was essential, one would suppose, that they should be chosen, as trustees are usually chosen, with regard to their fitness for the office. In fact, that was true of just 22 out of the 545 persons who were fellows of Oxford colleges in 1850. The rest were all of them holders of 'close' fellowships, reserved for persons with special quali- fications—e.g. men who had been born in the Province of Canterbury, or in the Diocese of Lincoln, or in the County of Dorset, or not more than fifty miles from Knaresborough, or in the parish where the Founder had been born himself.

If a satisfactory candidate with such qualifications did not present himself, the fellows were usually empowered to elect any unqualified candidate who was *habilis*, which was in practice interpreted as meaning suitable in their eyes to be a fellow. Any question as to qualifications or suitability would be decided by the Visitor.

Only two colleges, Balliol and Oriel, offered fellowships free from restrictions on candidature, to be awarded on an examination that was a real test of merit or of promise.

The result was, as one observer put it, that 'men who are naturally fitted to be country clergymen are bribed, because they were born in some parish in Rutland, to remain in Oxford until they are not only unfit for that, but for everything else'.

The system of close fellowships had made sense, of a rather haphazard sort, when communications between different parts of the country were difficult and people tended to live in or near the places where they were born; it did operate so as to spread the fellows, so to speak, more or less equitably over the country. But increasing ease of travel, particularly in the age of railways, was making nonsense of that system long before 1850.

The real trouble, however, was not the system itself but the spirit prevailing among those who administered it. For the system had become in many respects a dead letter, the colleges paying no more regard to the restrictions imposed by the Statutes than it suited them to do. Fellows were no longer *pauperes et indigentes*; kinship to the Founder now meant little or nothing; the colleges did not fulfil the religious purposes for which they had been created; the idea of the fellows as a resident body had quite disappeared. So, with restrictions on Fellowships: electors could in effect open the field to such candidates as they pleased by declaring the qualified candidates to be *non habiles* or simply passing them over in favour of a candidate that they preferred. If their proceedings were challenged, they could depend upon support from their episcopal Visitors.

What mattered, was the use they made of this power, what kind of people they elected; and that depended upon the tone and spirit that prevailed in the Governing Bodies of colleges. If they had all been like Oriel and Balliol, they could, in spite of their antiquated Statutes, have filled the Common Rooms of Oxford with keen scholars and stimulating teachers. But if all you were looking for was a congenial fourth at whist, you could probably find one who was born not more than fifty miles from Knaresborough; failing that, you simply looked further afield; an examination into intellectual and scholarly abilities would have been a positive embarrassment. If you were asked why you did not throw your fellowships open to talent, you took refuge behind the requirements of your Statutes and appealed to the sacredness of the intentions of the Founder.

To make reform more difficult, most (if not all) College Statutes contained a self-locking device, which preserved their requirements from ever being relaxed even by those who might be genuinely eager to amend them: the only persons (apart from the Legislature) that could alter them were the fellows, and the Statutes themselves regularly required that every fellow, on his appointment, should take an oath that he would not propose or accept (some Statutes added 'or permit') any alteration of their provisions.

That was a deadlock that only parliamentary legislation could break, and when Parliament did interfere in 1854 it repealed the provisions contained in College Statutes concerning such oaths, released fellows from the obligations already imposed by them, and prohibited the inclusion of any such provisions in College Statutes for the future. This made it possible for Statutes to be altered, for restrictions on fellowships to be removed, and—if a proper spirit prevailed in the elections—for the ablest candidates, henceforward, to be elected fellows.

The opportunity for the voices of the reformers to make themselves heard came in 1850, when Lord John Russell moved in the House of Commons for the appointment of a Royal Commission 'to inquire into the state, discipline, studies and revenues of the University and Colleges of Oxford'. Mr Gladstone, who may be taken as representing moderate opinion in the University, opposed the motion in a long and persuasive speech, maintaining that Oxford was well aware of the need for reform and perfectly ready to carry out the necessary measures without the intervention of Parliament. The proposal, however, was generally welcomed in Oxford, except by the forces of reaction— the Heads of Houses (other than Dr Jeune, the Master of Pembroke, who was ostracized by his fellow-Heads for accepting a seat on the Commission) and the ecclesiastical party, led by Dr Pusey and J. W. Burgon.

In spite of opposition within Oxford and without, and in spite of strenuous attempts to prove that the Crown had no legal power to inquire into the Universities, the Bill was passed and a Commission was set up in August 1850.

The Commission began its investigations in the autumn. It addressed to the Vice-Chancellor and to the Heads of Houses, and also to the professors and public officers and 'other eminent Persons connected with the University', a series of searching questions, which covered the whole range of the topics then giving rise to controversy in Oxford: the government of the University, the restrictions on elections to fellowships and the conditions attaching to them, the system of college lecturing and the practice of going to private coaches, the expediency of combining the professorial with the tutorial system, and the great problem of university extension—'the means of extending the benefits of the University to a larger number of students'.

The Vice-Chancellor and a number of the colleges boycotted the inquiry, which had no power to compel evidence, and Christ Church did not even acknowledge the communication addressed to it; but enough witnesses contributed to make the report and the evidence appended to it the fullest and most interesting account there is of Oxford in the nineteenth century. Pattison was among those who offered evidence.[1]

On the main question, that of the close fellowships, the almost unanimous opinion of the witnesses was summed up by Frederick Temple:

Of all the reforms in Oxford, this appears to me to be the vital one. Without a thorough reform here, all other reforms are as likely as not to be mischievous, for the skill to use them will be wanting. With a thorough reform here, all others become of less importance, for they are sure at last to follow. No corporate body is really reformed till its ablest men are put at the head of it. The fellows have become the head of the University and

[1] Evidence was submitted in writing. Among the professors who contributed were Nassau Senior, Herman Merivale, Halford Vaughan, and Conington, and the 'eminent persons' included A. H. Clough, Robert Lowe, Jowett, E. A. Freeman and Frederick Temple, besides Pattison himself.

cannot now be dislodged... The nation is bound to see that they are the ablest men that the University can supply.

On the question of the professoriate the Commissioners found an equally overwhelming consensus of opinion:'To represent fully the feeling in Oxford in favour of creating an effective Professoriate [they said] would be to reprint a portion of the evidence of almost every gentleman who had communicated with us.'

'Almost every gentleman': but they treated with great respect the most notable exception, Pattison. He was the only liberal who argued that there should be no increase in the number and importance of the professors.

Everyone, or almost everyone, admitted the inadequacy of the college tutorial system; and everyone, or almost everyone, agreed that the obviously right way to supplement it was not by private unofficial coaching but by instruction provided by the University through professors and assistant-professors or readers and lecturers—and that in fact was what the Commission ultimately recommended in its Report.

The main opposition to professors came from those— there were plenty of them in Oxford, then as now—who were constitutionally averse to change of any kind, 'the men [as Pattison put it] who resist alteration as such, not because they perceive that its scope will be mischievous, but because they cannot comprehend its scope at all'. There were, of course, plenty of people who were ready to paint a ridiculous picture of a married professoriate filling the courts and quadrangles with perambulators containing the professorial offspring; others feared professors as the advance guard of the natural sciences; while the fiercest opposition came from those who, like Pusey, regarded the professor as a propagator of infidelity and scepticism, and saw in German scholarship a danger to the Church.

It might at first sight seem strange to find Pattison, always a radical and a reformer, and already on the way to becoming a religious sceptic, in that sort of company.

If you look at his evidence, however, you will see that he takes a standpoint quite his own. He uses none of the stock arguments against the professoriate—indulges in no cheap gibes about 'outlandish subjects', makes no appeals *ad terrorem* about the danger of innovation or about infidelity and the threat to the Church, never depreciates 'useless' learning or cries down the physical sciences as illiberal.

Instead, you will find a sustained argument designed to prove the necessity in higher education of a personal relationship between the teacher and the taught. Professorial lectures, he says, are in place at Mechanics' Institutes, to convey the elements of knowledge to youthful or ignorant hearers, or in metropolitan lecture-halls, to exhibit a superficial view of a serious subject before a fashionable audience. For the student, the serious student in the higher reaches of learning, what is needed is the immediate contact of mind with mind; instruction, at those levels, is a voyage of discovery undertaken by the teacher in company with the taught; the catechetical lecture of the college lecture-room is the best vehicle for such instruction,[1] and

---

[1] The lectures given by college lecturers at this time were called 'catechetical'; they were really 'classes', in which the lecturer expounded a text and pupils might be put on to 'construe', as in a schoolroom.

the best kind of instructor is the college lecturer, or, failing an efficient college lecturer, the private coach. 'The mischief of the Professorial system', he declares, 'is that it implies a different idea of education; that it aims at, and is the easiest and readiest way to, a very inferior stamp of mental cultivation, but a cultivation which from its showy, available marketable character, is really an object of ambition in an age like the present.'

If you want to see the kind of cultivation that is generated by professorial lectures, by the lectures of the lecture-tour, or by set lectures like, say, the Clark Lectures, you will find it, according to Pattison, in America and in France, where there is a high standard of technical education and a wide spread of superficial general information—a smattering of culture.

I have no wish [he says] to depreciate this species of education, which I would willingly see much more widely diffused in this country, but in its proper sphere—for the classes, that is, whose callings in life will not admit of the more protracted process which a solid education requires...Each system has its own place; they should not be rivals; the one for the mass of the people, the other for a cultivated clerisy. If the University can do anything by the way for the diffusion and popularization of knowledge, well and good; and this is the proper object of Professorial lecturing; but they should never lose sight of their higher functions, that of sustaining the student through a long course of painful and rigorous discipline of the intellect, towards which the Professor's chair can render little, if any, help.

Porro unum necessarium, he concluded: if you want to make Oxford teaching what it should be, what you must do, and all you need do, is to reform the system of close fellowships: throw the fellowships open to all comers and elect the fellows for their ability as scholars and as teachers, and the tutorial problem will have solved itself.

The other main topic of Pattison's submission was university extension. Of course he was in favour of it. 'The ideal of a national University is that it should be co-extensive with the nation—it should be the common source of the whole of the higher (or secondary) instruction for the country.' Fifteen hundred youths, scions of the aristocracy and the gentry, representatives of Matthew Arnold's 'Barbarian' stratum of English society, idling away three years before stepping into the family property or the family living or the family business—these were not an adequate population, in numbers or character, for a national university:

If we can only draft in 500, or say 300 students (additional) from a class whose education has hitherto terminated with the national school or the commercial academy, the good that would be effected by acting even on this moderate scale cannot be represented by figures. It would be the beginning of a system by which the University would strike its roots freely into the subsoil of society, and draw from it new elements of life, and sustenance of mental and moral power.[1]

[1] An effort in the direction of University extension had been made in 1846, when thirty-three distinguished persons, headed by Lords Sandon and Ashley and including Gladstone, Sidney Herbert, Sir Thomas Dyke Acland, and Samuel Wilberforce, presented an Address to the Hebdomadal Board suggesting 'the addition of new departments to existing Colleges, or, if necessary...the foundation of new collegiate bodies' which should be 'accessible to the sons of parents whose incomes are too narrow for the scale of expenditure at present prevailing among the junior members of the University of Oxford'. The proposers' aims, however, were very different from

On the wider consequences and implications of his views on university extension I shall have something to say later. At this point I want only to draw attention to the views that he presented to the Commission in 1850. Here, as on the issue of 'Tutors *v*. Professors', they were, surprisingly, less radical than those of the Commissioners themselves, and here again the reason was to be found in his own experience as a college tutor.

If you wanted, as Pattison wanted, to increase the undergraduate population, the first obstacle to be overcome was the requirement that every undergraduate must belong to and reside in a college or established hall. Since living in

Pattison's; what they had in mind was not to make Oxford a more truly 'national' university, but simply to provide more qualified candidates for ordination. There was, they pointed out, 'a chasm which needs to be filled' between 'the ministry, which requires to be augmented' and the provision made by existing church schools and associations for such augmentation. They concluded by offering 'to aid by our personal exertions, or pecuniary contributions, in the promotion of a design which the exigencies of the country so clearly seem to require'.

The Board referred the Address to a Committee, whose Report (a beautiful specimen of its kind) is printed as Appendix E to the Evidence of the 1850 Commission. They declared that there was still room in the Colleges for additional students; that undergraduate expenses were not excessive, and had been reduced, and that the authorities were in any event powerless to check extravagance where it existed; that there were a number of arguments (duly rehearsed) why the foundation of new institutions was difficult and inexpedient and likely to fail of its purpose; and that they were 'not prepared to recommend any relaxation of the existing statutable restrictions upon the residence of candidates without the walls of Collegiate buildings'. In short, nothing need or could be done. Nevertheless, they concluded, 'there is ample room for the exertions of benevolence and liberality' and they, in effect, invited the would-be reformers to spend their money in helping the Board to keep things as they were.

college was more expensive than living in lodgings, and since the number of those that could be accommodated within college walls was limited, this requirement imposed a twofold restriction upon the 'intake' of the University. Three remedies were proposed: first, to build more independent halls of residence; second, to permit members of a college to lodge outside its walls; third, to admit to the University unattached students, members of neither a college nor a hall. These remedies were not mutually exclusive and the Commission was in favour of them all. Pattison drew the line at the last: he was opposed to the admission of unattached, non-collegiate, students. Here again he was not swayed by conventional arguments; he was not impressed by the supposed dangers to morals of allowing young men to 'live out'—'the practice at Cambridge' said W. C. Lake 'of allowing undergraduates to reside in the town, is said to produce a great deal of immorality (particularly among female servants)'—nor by the suggestion that 'living out' would dissolve a supposed pastoral relation between the college tutor and his pupil; he was, indeed, in favour of the undergraduates being allowed to live in lodging-houses; what he insisted on was that they must belong to a college so that they might have the intellectual guidance of a college tutor. 'I have been arguing against the boarding system, not against the collegiate system...Scheme No. (3) (for unattached students) would be nothing less than the substitution of the Professorial for the tutorial system—of the University for the Colleges...It would be virtually destroying a peculiar and most valuable feature of the English Universities.'

It is not difficult to see how Pattison came to take the attitude he displayed in his evidence, both in regard to the Professoriate and in regard to non-Collegiate students, and why he maintained it with such ardour: it was the result of his own experience—his experience as an undergraduate at Oriel, when he longed in vain for intellectual companionship and guidance, and his experience as a tutor at Lincoln, when he was able to supply that guidance to others, and to prove how much could be done for the expanding intellect by close companionship with a superior mind in the pursuit of knowledge.

Pattison submitted his evidence to the Commission in the spring or summer of 1851.[1] In the autumn there supervened a crisis in his life: the issue of reform *versus* reaction was put to the test within the walls of his own College.

In Lincoln Pattison was, of course, the leader of the younger fellows against the seniors and the Rector; the juniors, he said, formed 'an opposition that contended for discipline, decency, order, and religion (outward)'. But they were always outvoted by the seniors, with the Rector and his casting-vote. The old gang (as he described them) 'could fetch up from no great distance—Northampton—another wretched *crétin* of the name of Gibbs, who was always glad to come and booze at the College port a week or two when his vote was needed in support of old abuses'.

During the summer the Rector of Lincoln fell ill, and it was plain that he was going to die.

[1] All the evidence given to the Commission was submitted in writing, and hardly any of it is dated in the Report.

So the scene was set, in the autumn of 1851, on the small stage of Lincoln, for a drama exciting in itself and of symbolic interest for the whole University. Cast for the part of hero was Pattison, the leader of reform in a college that was a prize example of the old close-fellowship abuses. He had 'invested his whole heart and pride' in Lincoln; if he became its Head, he would not only achieve a commanding position within its walls, but as a member of the Hebdomadal Board he would join the oligarchy that governed Oxford. So he might help to realize the ideals he had testified to earlier in the year before Lord John Russell's Commission.

The Rector died at the beginning of the Michaelmas Term and was buried on 29 October. The election of his successor was fixed for 13 November. In the intervening fortnight there ensued a drama that is recounted in detail in Pattison's *Memoirs*, the action of which I can only summarize.

If Pattison was cast for the part of hero, the villain was a non-resident fellow, a Chancery barrister, J. L. R. Kettle. To appreciate the importance of Kettle, one must examine the voting situation on the eve of the election. One of the twelve fellowships was vacant, and two of the eleven fellows were out of the country; that left nine effective voters. Pattison had his own vote and the votes of the three junior fellows. Four other voters belonged to the old reactionary rump. The ninth, and deciding, vote was Kettle's. On the evening of the Rector's funeral, Kettle, who was himself a strong reformer and a keen critic of the close fellowship system, promised his vote to Pattison.

'You understand', Pattison told him, 'that this gives me the election.'

The only candidate in the field for the rectorship besides Pattison was 'old' Kay, an ex-fellow who for ten years had been mouldering in a Yorkshire living; he was odious to Pattison's party not only as an enemy to reform, but because they believed him to be under the influence of Richard Michell, an ex-fellow, now Vice-Principal of Magdalen Hall, who was a personal enemy of Pattison. Michell was determined, so Pattison's party believed, to run the College himself, using Kay as a puppet. Kay represented the old *régime*, and he could count on the votes of the four senior fellows. With Kettle's vote on their side, however, Pattison's party were sure to defeat Michell's machinations by a majority of one.

This being the state of affairs, it is easy to imagine the dismay of Pattison's supporters when, on the very eve of the election, Kettle, who had come down from London on the afternoon train (it was in those days the 4.50, reaching Oxford at 6.20) and put up at the Mitre, informed Pattison that he was now pledged to vote for Kay. Michell, it appeared, had secretly persuaded him a few days before that Kay, in his remote Yorkshire parsonage, had somehow become a convert to the cause of university reform. Michell had kept this supposed conversion dark from Kay's Conservative supporters, reassuring them that their candidate was as staunch a supporter as ever of the *status quo*.

In the face of this defection, what were Pattison and his party to do? His own cause was evidently a lost one, and the election was to take place at 10 o'clock on the following morning. Men less devoted to the cause of reform might have despaired. Not they. The vote of one of the rump might be detached from Kay if a suitable alternative candidate could be found. One of the senior fellows, Washbourne West, had been heard to say that the man he would like best to see as Rector was Thompson, an ex-Fellow who held the College living of Cublington. Perhaps West could be persuaded that his promise to vote for Kay was really conditional, and would not be binding on him if Thompson were brought into the field as a candidate. Their council lasted till after midnight; they decided that it was worth making the attempt.

At 3 o'clock in the morning, therefore, Pattison's supporters knocked up West and promised him that if he would vote for Thompson, they would do the same; and at the meeting, to the utter surprise and discomfiture of Kettle, Thompson was carried in by the five votes of West and the Pattison party.

What kind of person was the new Rector? 'It was impossible', according to Pattison, 'to say anything in defence of him. He was a mere ruffian.' Again: 'It was a return to the reign of the satyrs and wild beasts. Thompson was nothing better than a satyr.' A less prejudiced observer, John Morley, who was an undergraduate at Lincoln in the 'sixties, describes him as a 'grotesque divine, [whose] manners, bearing, and accomplishments were more fitted for the porter of a workhouse than the Head of a college'.[1]

---

[1] Even his literacy was called in question: it was doubted whether he could read and write—and these doubts were only partially allayed when, shortly after his election, a notice in his own hand was posted

Such was the man—a relic of the Lincoln of the unregenerate days—whom the party that stood for reform and enlightenment carried into office rather than have imposed on them the candidate put forward by the other side.

The disaster, as we shall see, crushed Pattison for the time being and had in the long run a decisive influence on his ideas concerning university reform. Its effect upon the reputation of Lincoln College and the reforming party in Oxford was immediate.

The dirty linen was well washed in public. Kettle addressed an open letter to Thompson, in which he printed private correspondence intended for college eyes alone (a manoeuvre that men not of the highest honour sometimes resort to when disappointed in their aims), suggesting that the successful party had acted from interested motives —they voted for Thompson, he alleged, because Thompson had a college living to resign, which meant a benefit to the fellows—and presenting the whole episode as an example of the evils that were bound to arise under a system of close fellowships.

Kettle concluded his letter by expressing his bitter regret (surely here there was a touch of hypocrisy?) that the public gaze should have been 'so strongly attracted to the degraded state of our College'. His only consolation, he says, 'arises from the hope that the monstrous evil of close Fellowships in the University will now be apparent',

in the College Lodge. The notice, said the undergraduates, was certainly evidence of the Rector's ability to write; whether or not he could read was still an open question.

and he suggested that Thompson himself should take the lead 'in promoting those reforms which will enable us to choose a higher class of men in the future'. There was a counter-pamphlet by a supporter of Pattison; he vigorously repudiated Kettle's imputation of corrupt motives to the successful party, but he was handicapped in defending their course of action because he naturally could not confess the motive that had in fact inspired it—the desire to ensure that, if Pattison had to be defeated, at least his enemies should be deprived of the fruits of victory.

A junior member of the College[1] weighed in with *The Mysteries of the Lincoln Common Room Unveiled*, taking a line strongly favourable to Pattison and placing the other actors in the drama in a farcical light: 'One moment a disappointed candidate retires, carpet bag in hand, to the Mitre, to eat the sandwich of despair, whilst an elated rival has already ordered his traps and a haunch of mutton to the Rectory.' The anonymous author ended on a more serious note, assuring his readers that Pattison's pupils, 'past and present, are *unanimous* in the feeling and expression of their esteem and attachment', and describing him as 'the man who commanded popularity without stooping to court it, who made his friends by strictly and

[1] Henry Whitehead, who had taken his B.A. the year before. I suspect that Whitehead may also have been 'Lincolniensis', the author of a letter to the newspapers dated 'Oxford, Nov. 28', which takes up the cudgels for Pattison as a tutor, and concludes with a shrewd hit at Kettle himself, the non-resident fellow: 'Be careful, how you make charges which can be so easily retorted, and remember that whenever that Reform, of which you profess yourself a zealous and consistent advocate, shall be effected, its first measure will be to put an end to a position so useless and anomalous as your own.'

faithfully discharging his duties, and his foes by preferring the interests of his College to—"social parties" and "unexceptionable port"'.

But the last word was with Kettle. He had lost no time in appealing to the Visitor, the Bishop of Lincoln, against the validity of Thompson's election. The Visitor dismissed the appeal, but he appended to his decision an admonitory memorandum that was much to Kettle's purpose, and Kettle determined to make use of it. *Flectere si nequeo superos, Acheronta movebo*: having failed to carry the day among his colleagues, he would see if he could harm the College by damaging its reputation in the eyes of the Commission of Inquiry. He therefore forwarded the Visitor's pronouncement to the Commissioners with a covering letter of his own, in the hope that they would print these documents among the evidence appended to their Report. He was only just in time. His letter was dated 20 April 1852. The Commissioners were putting the finishing touches to their work; their final meeting was held on Friday, 23 April, and they signed the Report four or five days later.

The Report and Evidence came out in August in a bulky folio—the great Blue Book that was by the bedside of the Chancellor, the Duke of Wellington, the night before his death on 14 September—'I shall never get through it, Charles', he said to his son before retiring for the night, 'but I must work on'. If the Duke had got through it, he would have found, upon the very last of its eight hundred pages, Kettle's letter printed in full, together with the admonition of the Visitor. Kettle's letter called attention to 'the actual state of one of the Colleges which elect their Fellows on close principles' and to 'the low moral tone which prevails in such Societies, and the unscrupulous determination to sacrifice all other objects to their own preferment', and the Bishop declared that he felt it 'his painful duty to observe, that although [the Visitor] finds no sufficient ground in the statements which have been laid before him for pronouncing that corrupt practices have prevailed at the above-mentioned election, yet, looking at what passed...he finds much which is calculated to reflect little credit on the College'.

So the episode was made, albeit at the expense of the reformers, to serve the cause of university reform.

4

THE IDEA OF A UNIVERSITY

An American author who was entertained at the Oxford Commemoration in the summer of 1877 referred obliquely in a characteristic passage to the question of university reform. After the Encaenia ceremony, says Henry James, 'I was invited to a lunch-party at the particular College at which I should find it the highest privilege to reside. I may not' (he mysteriously adds) 'further specify it.' He does, however, mention that 'it is deemed by persons of a reforming turn of mind the best appointed abuse in a nest of abuses', and, in case that does not suffice for identification, he adds that it is the one Oxford college at which there are no undergraduates. He continues: 'A Commission for the expurgation of the universities has lately been appointed by Parliament to look into it—a Commission armed with a gigantic broom, which is to sweep away all the fine old ivied and cobwebbed improprieties.'[1]

The Commission had been set up by Lord Salisbury earlier in the year, and the task set it was to inquire into 'the main purposes relative to the University for which provision should be made, the sources from which funds for those purposes should be obtained; and the principles on

[1] See James's *Portraits of Places* (1883), pp. 244–6, for a characteristic and perceptive sketch of All Souls, and an appraisal of 'the peculiar air of Oxford—the air of liberty to care for intellectual things, assured and secured by machinery which is in itself a satisfaction to sense'.

which payments from the Colleges for those purposes should be contributed'.

Lord John Russell's Commission, twenty-five years before, had concentrated its attention on the 'state, discipline, and studies' of the University; now attention was to be directed towards its finances,[1] and the issue was the redistribution of college endowments. That raised—as inquiries about endowments so often do—fundamental questions: what (in particular) was the *raison d'être* of an academic establishment? How were the demands of learning to be harmonized with the demands of education? Against the background of this inquiry, the rival claims of the colleges and the University were again brought into conflict.

Mark Pattison, in the evidence he submitted to the Commission of 1850, had stood forth, almost alone among the liberals, and with an uncongenial ally in Dr Pusey, as a passionate champion of the college against the University, of the tutors against the professors.

In 1877 he appeared in the opposite *rôle*, championing the professors against the tutors, and the University as an institution for learning against the college as an establishment for education.

The new Commission was presided over by Lord Selborne; to take evidence, it met in Oxford; and since the University had no suitable offices to put at its disposal—a

[1] Into which a preparatory inquiry had been made, in great detail, by a Commission, which was appointed by Mr Gladstone, and of which the Duke of Cleveland was chairman, in 1872–4.

symptom of the academic poverty that it was the Commission's function to investigate—its sittings took place in
the Clarendon Hotel. Pattison gave his evidence on
2 November. The last question put to him before he left
the room was asked by Lord Redesdale, who up to that
point in the proceedings had remained silent. It was this:

Do you consider that the great object of a University ought to
be to produce the greatest number of useful members of
society, whereby the nation at large may be most extensively
benefited?

Pattison's answer was 'Certainly'. Of course, it had to
be; no witness could afford to answer that question in the
negative. And, in fact, Pattison meant what he said. But
his answer needed explanation. His 'Certainly' might have
seemed to commit him, in contradiction to the tenor of all
his previous replies, to a view of the University, like
Jowett's, as a training-ground for legislators, adminis-
trators, diplomatists, country magistrates, useful citizens.
What he would have liked to say, no doubt, was 'Yes,
but—' and to have gone on to explain, first, what he
meant by benefiting the nation at large, and then what he
meant by education, expounding at length his opinion of
the true function of a university.

To appreciate all that was involved in the position that
Pattison finally assumed, we must take into account what
had happened to him, and what had happened to Oxford,
since he submitted evidence to Lord John Russell's
Commission a quarter of a century earlier.

What had happened in that interval to Pattison himself?
What had transformed the eager tutorial fellow, 'his whole

heart and pride invested in his college', into the disillusioned head of that same college, who said 'it is by not
caring that I live'?

First, of course, there was the great turning-point of his
life—his failure to achieve the Rectorship of Lincoln in 1851.
In the course of ten years' labour as a devoted and successful
college tutor, he had built up a tower of hopes, for himself
and for his college, and the whole structure, as the result
of one night's work, had come crashing to the ground. I
will not stop to inquire whether he need have taken it as
hardly as he did. A different man, no doubt, would have
gone to work again, conciliated the new Rector, maintained
his own dominance in the society, and kept his college in
the forefront of its rivals. But Pattison was not such a man.
He collapsed; he was prostrated. 'The crash', he wrote to
his sisters a couple of days after the *débacle*, 'as far as my
academical career is concerned is utter, complete, and
hopeless. The College, for my time, is extinguished...I
can forgo easily', he continued, 'the station and externals,
but the sphere for my practical energies which is gone
cannot be replaced. You cannot exaggerate the wretched
state in which I have been ever since—and the pain of the
heartache which I cannot subdue. We have all here lost
something—but no-one has lost what I have lost—all
earthly hopes.'

The language sounds exaggerated, but it was matched by
his physical reaction: 'My mental forces', he wrote in his
Memoirs, 'were paralysed by the shock; a blank, dumb
despair filled me; a chronic heartache took possession of
me, perceptible even through sleep. As consciousness

returned in the morning, it was only to bring with it a livelier sense of the cruelty of the situation into which I had been brought.'

The process of recovery was very gradual. He turned to Nature to repair the ravages of the college election. About the middle of April, after long and anxious preparation of rods and tackle, with a box of books and a large store of tobacco, he used to set out for solitude. He fished the streams of his native Swaledale; thence he pushed on to the waters of the Border and beyond. He would return to Oxford for a few weeks in the middle of the Long Vacation. When September came, he would set off for a ramble in Germany. He travelled on foot, delighting in the discovery of nooks and corners unknown to guide-books. When he returned to College, he kept himself to himself. To the undergraduates of that day he was a solemn and mysterious figure.

He spoke to no one [wrote John Morley in later years], saluted no one, and kept his eyes steadily fixed on infinite space. He dined at the high table, but uttered no word. He never played the part of host, nor did he ever seem to be a guest...He was a complete stranger in the college. We looked upon him with the awe proper to one who was supposed to combine bound-less erudition with an impenetrable misanthropy. In reading the fourth book of the Ethics, we regarded the description of the High-souled Man, with his slow movements, his deep tones, his deliberate speech, his irony, his contempt for human things ...as the model of the inscrutable sage in the rooms under the clock.

Pattison's disappointment, as it drove him in on himself, also cut him off from the life of Oxford. While he devoted himself to learning, he abandoned teaching; he resigned his college tutorship, and took no further interest in the success of Lincoln in the Schools.

Nor did he engage in the administrative business of the University. He did allow himself to be put up for the new Hebdomadal Council on two occasions; but 'fortunately for me', he says, 'I was left in a minority each time, or I might have wasted years in the idle and thankless pursuit which they call doing university business'. I do not think that this was a case of sour grapes. 'I am fairly entitled to say', he went on, 'that since the year 1851, I have lived wholly for study. There can be no vanity', he added, 'in making this confession, for, strange to say, in a university ostensibly endowed for the cultivation of science and letters, such a life is hardly regarded as a creditable one.'

His self-imposed exile from practical affairs had another result: he spent much of his time abroad; in particular he paid frequent visits to Germany, staying on into the winter, and settling at some university. In 1856, for instance, he attended courses at Heidelberg.

In 1858 he spent several months as *The Times* correspondent in Berlin, and in the following year he went out as an inspector, specially appointed by the Education Committee of the Privy Council to report on the state of elementary education in Prussia and the German states.

In Germany Pattison saw in action a type of university totally different from Oxford and Cambridge—the university in which every subject and every branch of every subject in the field of knowledge was explored;

where each was represented by a professor or more than one professor; where students boarded by themselves in the town, and the college and the college tutor were things unheard of; and where the place of the tutorial hour and the catechetical lecture of the Oxford and Cambridge system was taken by the seminar conducted by the professor with a few chosen pupils. Apart from this, instruction was given entirely by means of professorial lectures, supplemented of course by the reading of books.

There was not much romance about such a university—no 'fine old ivied improprieties'; but there was an atmosphere in which learning was respected by all and ardently pursued by student and teacher.

It was just at this time that an outside observer, with experience of both Germany and England, Ernest Renan, painted a vivid picture of the minor German university, with its narrow way of life, its starved, uncouth, professors, and its slave-driven *Privatdozenten*; such a university, he went on to say, 'does more for the human spirit than the aristocratic University of Oxford with its princely revenues, its magnificent college buildings, its opulent style of living and its idle Fellows'.

'A brilliant lecture-list', said Pattison, 'is a paper issue which may, or may not, be redeemable at par'; but it is, as he went on to point out, an indication of the range and vitality of studies in a university. At a date when reformers in Oxford were vainly trying to increase the number of professorships to something like fifty (in 1850 the total number of professorships in the University was only 25 with about a score of readerships and praelectorships) and to secure a place in the curriculum for the physical sciences and modern languages, Leipzig, a university less than half the size of Oxford, had more than a hundred professors on its books (Curtius and Tischendorff among them), each of them delivering at least two courses of lectures on subjects ranging from Modern Arabic to Practical Economics, with the Comparative Philology of the Romance Languages and Psychiatry and Aesthetics thrown in.

True, professors in Germany were underpaid, and in most states could be dismissed at the will of the government. But, instead of being ridiculed and despised, as they were in Oxford, they were held in honour. Halford Vaughan, the Regius Professor of Modern History, in a pamphlet defending the Oxford professoriate,[1] reminded the Hebdomadal Board of the rebuke administered by Alexander von Humboldt to the Elector of Hanover: the Elector had observed that 'there are two classes of persons who can always be had for payment—Huren und Professoren'; 'As to the first class', said Humboldt, 'I bow to your Majesty's authority; as to the second, to have been a half-Professor is the glory of my life.'

The difference between the regard in which learning was held in Germany and in England can be measured statistically. In or about the year 1860 the numbers of undergraduates attending the universities in Prussia, the other German states, and the Austrian Empire, together amounted to about 18,000, out of a population of some 50 millions. The population of England and Wales at that

---

[1] *Oxford Reform and Oxford Professors* (1854).

date was just over 20 millions; the undergraduates at Oxford and Cambridge together numbered hardly 3,000 —six times as many students in Germany out of a population little more than twice as large.

Even more striking was the difference between the attitudes of English and German students towards their work. Matthew Arnold, who inspected German universities for the Schools Inquiry Commission in 1865, gave it as his verdict that the fundamental ideas of the German system were *Lehrfreiheit* and *Lernfreiheit*—liberty for the teacher and liberty for the learner—and *Wissenschaft*, science, knowledge, systematically pursued and prized in and for itself. And here is Max Müller describing to Lord Salisbury's Commission the experience of one who had been a student in Germany and was now a professor in Oxford:

The great difference to me between the German and English universities is that I see that the three years of his academic life are to a German student years of intense enjoyment and pleasure; he rushes to the lectures; he is drawn by curiosity; he wants to hear the best professors. I do not mean to say that he always works very hard, but whatever he does he does of his own free will, and he enjoys it. He is not always told: at eight o'clock you must do this, at nine o'clock you must read that book, at ten o'clock you must go to that tutor, and at eleven o'clock you must produce that essay. When he works, it is a pleasure to him to work...I only want to give the Commission the different impression that is conveyed to me by German and English students. I hardly ever hear a German student grumble, but on the contrary he likes his three years; he likes not simply the bodily athletics but the intellectual athletics of the place. As a rule that is not the case at Oxford, and I believe that that is due to the constant pressure and supervision of tuition which is experienced here, and therefore although upon the subject itself which is taught the amount of learning carried away from the university may be very much the same in Germany as in England, yet the character of it and the feeling with which one looks back to it is different.

During the ten years from 1851 onwards Pattison underwent a conversion—a conversion from Oxford to Germany, from teaching to learning. At the end of the decade, in 1861, there came another turning-point in his life: in January of that year he became head of his college; in September he married. He was forty-seven, and he was now, as he says, possessed of 'unrivalled academic leisure'. For the rest of his life—and he still had nearly a quarter of a century to live—he could observe Oxford from the windows of the Rector's Lodgings with a detached and critical gaze.

As he looked down from those windows during the 'sixties and 'seventies Pattison saw a very different kind of university from that which had existed in the days of the Commission of 1850. A man who had left the University in 1845 and returned to it fifteen years later would hardly have recognized it as the same place: the Oxford of Dr Arnold had become the Oxford of Matthew Arnold; the Oxford of Verdant Green had become the Oxford of T. H. Green.

This metamorphosis was due to the success of the reforms for which Pattison and his fellow-liberals had striven in the 1840s. It was the great Blue Book of 1852, the Report of Lord John Russell's Commission, that had wrought the change—or, at least, that had made it possible.

The weight of the arguments contained in that Report had made a notable convert: Mr Gladstone, who as a member for the University had in 1850 opposed the setting up of the Commission, moved the Bill giving effect to its recommendations that became the Oxford University Act of 1854. By that Act, and the machinery that it provided, the whole face of Oxford was altered.

First, and most important, all restrictions on fellowships were abolished; the old close system, and the oaths incorporated in the College Statutes that made that system immutable, came to an end; colleges were obliged to award fellowships for merit demonstrated in examination. This was the vital change; over the next couple of decades it restocked the Common Rooms of Oxford with a new breed of don.

Before long, the private tutor or coach was dying out; he was no longer needed to do the work of the college tutor in training the ablest undergraduates to distinguish themselves in the Schools; the college tutors themselves were now busily engaged in doing that; the private coach ministered instead to those who were struggling for a pass. In that *rôle*, he lasted on into the present century; in my own day it was the backward or the idle, not the able and industrious, who had recourse to coaching.

Then, the curriculum was extended by the recognition of the claims of Science. In 1826 Dr Daubeny, the Professor of Chemistry, had had to pay for the fitting up of the University laboratories out of his own pocket; the old Hebdomadal Board refused to allow him to be reimbursed by the University. Now, in 1859, the University erected a magnificent Museum devoted entirely to the physical sciences.

Then, in the 'sixties, an inroad was made on the old inclosed system of college lecturing: inter-collegiate lectures were instituted, with such success that the professors (whose numbers had been increased, the new Chairs being paid for out of the suppressed fellowships) began to complain that they were being robbed of their audiences.

The college system was further eroded when undergraduates were allowed to live out of college and when there was established, in 1868, a Delegacy for Non-Collegiate Students. More students, and poor students, drawn in larger proportions from the commercial and professional classes, came up to Oxford, and they came up not simply to idle, but to work for a degree.

The range from which students were drawn was made still wider, and the clerical predominance in Oxford was undermined, by the abolition in the 'seventies of religious tests for matriculation and the B.A. degree, and of the requirement to take Orders that had attached to most fellowships.

Finally, the constitution of the University was remodelled: the power of the Heads of Houses was broken; the old Hebdomadal Board was replaced by a Council most of whose members were elected by Congregation, and the powers of Congregation were strengthened and its procedure was modernized. Oxford was on the way to becoming a democratically constituted body—both in the sense that its own resident graduate members had an increasing share in its government, and in the sense that its undergraduate population was drawn from an increasingly wide range of social classes.

All this should have pleased the reformer Pattison. 'Give us leave', he had appealed to the Commissioners of 1850, 'to do something: we in Oxford are weary of scheming, suggesting, and pamphleteering...Untie our hands and open our gates, and let us at least try if we can attract here, and can usefully deal with, that larger circle of youth whom we are told we ought to have here.' Oxford had now been given the scope and opportunity that Pattison and his friends had craved for.

Unfortunately, as he looked down from the windows of his Lodgings in Lincoln in the 'sixties, Pattison was not pleased with what he saw. The last state of the University was, in his eyes, worse than the first. True, it was no longer the torpid old Tory Oxford, full of inefficient tutors spending idle days and dissipated nights, conducting formal examinations and giving elementary lectures to idle and apathetic undergraduates. Oxford had woken up; it had set its house in order.[1] But what had it become? A cramming-shop (the word is Pattison's), where able and energetic tutors trained eager and intelligent pupils, who had been bought with scholarships, to obtain Honours in the Schools.

And this resulted directly from the reforms of the pre-

[1] 'The last twenty years', he wrote in his *Suggestions on Academical Organisation* (1868), 'have seen more improvement in the temper and teaching of Oxford than the three centuries since the Reformation'— and he attributed this to 'the Reform Bill of 1854', and particularly to the abolition of close fellowships that it enacted.

ceding half-century, from the remoulding of the Examination Statutes and the opening up of the closed fellowships. The examination for the degree of B.A. had become a real test (a test *of what*?—that was another question), organized so as to allow candidates to display distinction—or at least to obtain distinctions; it was necessary to work hard for honours, and honours were worth working for, because they gave a social *cachet* and a professional qualification. The result, in Pattison's view, was death to the object for which a university existed: the pursuit of mental culture.

'Little did we foresee', he wrote, 'that in thus reforming the system we were only giving another turn to the examination screw, which has been turned several times since, till it has become an instrument of mere torture which has made education impossible and crushed the very desire of learning.'

'My young friend', he said to a Lincoln undergraduate of the 'seventies who showed signs of a real interest in the Classics, 'I am very grieved to tell you that if you have come up to Oxford with the idea of getting knowledge, you must give that up at once. It is merely a race, to get through the examinations; you have time for nothing else. We have bought you, and we're running you for two plates, Mods and the Finals.' This was a theme he was never tired of repeating: Oxford had reformed itself so as to satisfy the desires of the public; in so doing, it incapacitated itself from fulfilling its proper aim: 'Public Opinion, not dissatisfied at the degradation of a University into a School', as he put it, 'is disposed still further to lower the level of instruction.' 'The number of those who seek

education by means of the University is very small com-
pared with the number of those who seek the degree and
the social status it confers.'

University extension had merely opened the gates of
Oxford to a larger number of young men who came up
not to be educated, but to secure a degree. He lost patience
with them. 'You people come up here', he said in one such
case, 'and want all sorts of dispensations, and want our
scholarships, and want *us*. We don't want *you*—we don't
want *you*—we don't want *you*!'—and his voice, we are
told, 'rose at each repetition'.

'Here they come again!', he said, in mellower mood, as
he saw the undergraduates re-assembling at the beginning
of the term, 'Year after year, the same check suits! The
same horse-shoe tie-pins!'—and he sighed deeply.

Pattison was happier now in the smoking-room of the
Athenaeum than in the Common Room of Lincoln,
and more at home at a meeting of the Council of Bedford
College or of the Social Science Congress than at a college
meeting; Oxford was a 'desert of arid shop-dons'; a day
spent on College business was a day 'utterly wasted'; at the
beginning of term in January 1877 he entered in his diary,
'Term begins. Very low-spirited at the thought of the
weary round of busy, fussy, wasted hours.'

The democracy that now prevailed in the administra-
tion of university affairs was as hostile, he thought, to the
true aims of Oxford as was the race for degrees; the time
that the dons could spare from cramming their pupils for
the Schools was spent on the Boards and Committees of
the new self-governing university:

Young M.A.s of talent abound [he wrote in his *Memoirs*] but they are all taken up with the conduct of some wheel in the complex machinery of cram, which grinds down all specific tendencies and tastes into one uniform mediocrity. The men of middle age seem, after they reach thirty-five or forty, to be struck with an intellectual palsy, and betake themselves, no longer to port, but to the frippery work of attending boards and negotiating some phantom of legislation with all the importance of a cabinet council—*belli simulacra cientes*. Then they give each other dinners, where they assemble again with the comfortable assurance that they have earned their evening relaxation by the fatigues of the morning's committee. These are the leading men of our university, and who give the tone to it—a tone as of a lively municipal borough; all the objects of science and learning, for which a university exists, being put out of sight by the consideration of the material means of endowing them.

'The material means of endowing them': as the 'sixties went by, this question of endowments became more and more important in Oxford. With the extension of science, the increase in the professoriate, the creation of new lectureships and university offices, the expansion of libraries, museums, lecture rooms and examination rooms, it became plain that the University's revenues—a pitiful £30,000 a year—were utterly inadequate for its needs.

And it was plain also where the solution of the problem lay—it lay in the grotesquely disproportionate revenues of the colleges. Lord John Russell's Commission of 1850 had not ventured to suggest the redistribution of academical endowments. It was to investigate this problem that Lord Salisbury in 1877 appointed the Commission armed with the gigantic broom referred to by Henry James.

Before he gave his evidence to Lord Salisbury's Commission, Pattison had published two documents setting out his views on the question of endowments—in one, with great detail, in the other summarily.[1]

In 1868, he brought out his *Suggestions on Academical Organisation*—his recommendations for the reform of Oxford University. Later, in 1876, when Lord Salisbury's bill appointing a Commission was before Parliament, he contributed a short 'Review of the Situation' to a collection significantly entitled *Essays on the Endowment of Research*.

I can only reproduce here the barest outline of Pattison's Oxford blue-print. It was not a fantasy, a university in the air; it was his account of Oxford as he wanted it to be, and as it *could* be, worked out with due reference to pounds, shillings, and pence.

His programme was a radical one. It involved nothing less than the abolition of the colleges and the fellowships. The buildings would not, of course, be pulled down; but the corporations would be dissolved and their endowments transferred to the University. Nine of the colleges

[1] He had also published, in *Oxford Essays, contributed by Members of the University* (1855), an essay on 'Oxford Studies' in which he reviewed the situation immediately after the passing of the Oxford Reform Act of 1854: 'The Oxford Reform Act is now in operation', he wrote. 'It has not yet had time to fulfil or disappoint the hopes of its promoters or the fears of its opponents. But, within and without, there is a pause of expectation, balanced equally between hope and fear.' He himself was then full of hope; but he already perceived the dangers latent in reform: 'We should, however, be on our guard that we do not now...sacrifice the best minds to the necessity of stimulating the many. We must not over-examine or over-lecture the honour men.'

would become the headquarters of the nine Faculties, the senior professor being *ex officio* head of each. (The Law Faculty was allotted to the college so much favoured by Henry James.) The others would be kept on as halls of residence for those undergraduates who preferred a communal existence or, as Pattison scornfully put it, 'who come up to get the social stamp'.

Undergraduates would enrol with the University, and be allotted to a university tutor. There would be no entrance examination; any one could come into residence who could afford to. The cost of an Oxford education would be trifling. There would of course be no religious tests. There would be no pass degrees. No one need take the Schools if he did not wish to. Many, Pattison thought, would come into residence simply for love of learning; there would be no other reason for coming to Oxford.

The curriculum assumed that the student's general education was to be continued until Moderations—Classical or Mathematical and Physical—at the end of his first year at Oxford: thereafter he would embark on a truly advanced, specializing education, 'scientific' in the broader sense of the word, choosing, for the remainder of his time at the University, between the nine Faculties, which between them would cover the whole range of knowledge. At the end of his time he could, if he wished, be examined for a degree; but examinations would play a minor part in the process of education; they would be subordinated to the curriculum, instead of the curriculum being designed to fit the examinations; men would be examined in what they had learned in the course of accompanying the lecturers in their intellectual explorations; they would not spend their time 'learning' what they expected to be examined in.

Each of the nine Faculties would be autonomous, and would be staffed by a graduated professoriate—professors, assistant-professors, lecturers, tutors. They would be paid on a scale that would make the attainment of a Chair as desirable an object as success in any other profession.

The corner-stone of the whole edifice was the selection of the professoriate: there was to be no hint or possibility of patronage in their appointment; and they must be the best minds in the kingdom. All endowed appointments in the University should be made by a Board of five curators, themselves appointed by representatives of the Faculties: the curators would be drawn from the widest field inside or outside the University: the list of classes of persons who would be ineligible was characteristically Pattisonian: peers, sons of peers, members of the House of Commons, Bishops.

'The object of these Suggestions', Pattison concludes, 'is that the University shall no longer be a class-school, nor mainly a school for youth at all. It is a national institute for the preservation and tradition of useful knowledge. It is the common interest of the whole community that such knowledge should exist, should be guarded, treasured, cultivated, disseminated, expounded.'

Eight years after he published these *Suggestions*, in the 'Review of the Situation' that he contributed to *Essays on the Endowment of Research*, he reminded Lord Salisbury's Commission, who were shortly to commence their sittings, that, though their task ostensibly dealt only with finance, it concerned the fundamental purpose of the University. They would be dealing with large revenues, at present deployed in providing prize fellowships for sinecurists; were those revenues to be transferred to tutors, who—with or without the title of professor—would spend their time preparing students for examinations, or were they to endow a real professoriate, in which the occupant of every Chair was 'the master of his science and its representative before the world'?

'Shall we have a university', he concluded, 'to which free science and liberal letters attract, by their own lustre, only such ingenuous youth as have a true vocation; or shall we have a great national *lycée* through the routine of which we shall attempt to force willing and unwilling, apt and unapt alike, by the stimulus of emulation, of honours, prizes, and rewards?'[1]

Pattison knew very well that the institute for advanced study that he pleaded for must be, in the eyes of most people, a national luxury. To commend itself to the

[1] Pattison was not sanguine about the answer to this question; he feared that the outcome of a transfer of college revenues to the University would be, not the change he wanted, but a change for the worse; his fears are well expressed in a letter to Edward Appleton, editor of *The Academy*, which acted as an organ of the cause of the Endowment of Research: 'By continuing to work this point you may do much good, though I do not think you will be able to prevent a gigantic job which will soon be an avid contest here. The tutors are preparing to turn themselves into Professors! with permanent tenure, marriage, and increased salaries. In other words, the endowments of Oxford will go to pay tuition fees. Paterfamilias will get nothing; he will pay as before, and will receive the same article for his money which he did before, *et haec coquenda sunt nobis*!'

country at large a University must at least appear to equip citizens for some useful end in life. And that, incidentally, a University no doubt may do. Some will go to it for a general training to help them in their chosen profession, as others will to indulge their curiosity in a particular field of science or of humane learning. But, apart from such secondary functions, the existence of an institute of organized knowledge was, in Pattison's view, a possession that a nation should be just as proud of as it was of an academy of literature or the arts. The men who composed it might contribute no more towards meeting the nation's practical needs than do the artist, or the saint, or the athlete; but they enriched the nation by their very existence—for one of the measures of a nation's real wealth is the depth of its culture. And an association of such men, by the power of example, would breed newer generations like themselves.

Believing this, Pattison, when Lord Redesdale put to him in the Clarendon Hotel that ingeniously loaded question, could truthfully reply that the function of a University, as he saw it, was indeed 'to produce the greatest number of useful members of society, whereby the nation at large may be most extensively benefited'.

I have said that Pattison preached this doctrine with passion. He spoke with passion because he was speaking of what he knew. For fifty years, he said, he had lived for study. That was no less than the truth. I believe that he was supported through this sustained mental endeavour by a series of almost mystical experiences.

The Idea of a University

A. H. Sayce, in his *Reminiscences*, tells how on his first Sunday after coming into residence as an Oxford undergraduate in 1865, he attended both the morning and the afternoon service in the University Church, 'with all the zeal and innocence of a freshman'. He found it a puzzling experience. The morning sermon, which was preached by Pattison, concluded with the words (as Sayce recalled them): 'It will be an ill day for the Church of England when dogma and authority gain the upper hand and reason is denied its rightful place as the corner stone of all religion.'[1] In the afternoon, the preacher was Liddon. He began his sermon as follows: 'Dogma and authority, authority and dogma—these two form the keystone in the arch of our holy faith.' 'What', asked Sayce, 'was an innocent freshman to believe?' Pattison's sermon has survived in print; it was the last of a series of three University sermons preached at two-yearly intervals in 1861, 1863 and 1865. In them he developed systematically his ideas about the purpose of a university and in them he also displayed his deepest feelings on the subject.

I will try to convey the effect of those passages of his sermon in which Pattison seems to be speaking directly from his own experience. He begins by distinguishing 'the lower states of education...of which all men do or can partake', from 'the superior education which a University professes to administer'. In the first, the learner is passive; the education does not touch his mind. 'His

[1] His actual words (*Sermons*, 1885, p. 136) were, 'May [the Church of England] never take the fatal step of standing upon authority instead of upon reason, upon intellect, upon education, upon the spiritual and moral cultivation of the soul!'

understanding is exercised in bare apprehension of given facts and relations. His will is exercised in prompt obedience to a rule. His judgment consists in testing all his actions by this rule. He asks, What is customary? What does the Church say? What will people think? What are others doing?'

It is necessary and even salutary, Pattison says, to pass through this stage of education in order to fit ourselves for life: 'we must be incorporated into the social routine'. If that were the whole of life, if there were nothing behind phenomena, and if the reason were a purely passive faculty, education might end there. To instil such education is the function of elementary schools—and not only of elementary schools, but of all establishments that aim simply at dispensing knowledge or inculcating truth. Such establishments, in order to stimulate their pupils, have to rely on the promise of rewards and the fear of penalties. Oxford, in Pattison's opinion, by extending these aims and methods into the range of what should have been higher education, was degrading itself to the level of those Jesuit establishments that had for two centuries retarded the spread of reason and enlightenment over Europe. To him, the inculcation of dogma, religious or political, in establishments that professed to provide higher education was anathema. Today no doubt he would have found targets for his scorn not only in Rome but in Russia and 'emergent' Africa.

The faculty of reason, according to Pattison, is an active, questioning, faculty, and it is the business of the higher education not to suppress it or to harness it, as in the Jesuit and state-ridden schools, but to develop it. It should not be actuated, as in a school, by fear of punishment or desire of reward: the only stimulus it needs is the pleasure that a man feels in the consciousness of the development of his mind. Education must give full scope for this development, and so must be 'coextensive with the whole domain of thought'; it must 'recognise philosophy and religion' and not 'ignore philosophy and reduce religion to a system of arbitrary opinion, without a basis in the reason of things'. At this point in his sermon, Pattison launches out into what is for him an eloquent passage: as the mind is roused by superior education, he declares, it is no longer passive—

We perceive a new world underlying the world of sense, law, and custom; the material world recedes from our ken in its present immensity without limit in space, and in its past history without limit in time; the forces, electrical, chemical, gravitational, that govern the physical world, our own relations to the world around us...all this offers material of pressing importance for us to know, the material of a hundred sciences, a very small part of which can be exhausted in even the longest life. Then there is the social history of the race, in pre-historic periods; then written records from their commencement till now; political theory, the whole train of social evils and necessities loudly calling for aid and cure; art, literature, the history of the human spirit, place this [he concludes] and more, that cannot be enumerated—the *totum scibile*—before the mind's eye, and what human intellect does not feel over-whelmed by the enormity of the demand made upon it?... The finite understanding is crushed when it is brought into the presence of the infinite expanse of the knowable, and turns aside in despair.

At this point, he says—and surely he is writing here out of his own experience—a new light breaks in upon the learner:

He becomes conscious of a force within himself; he feels the stirring of an innate power unknown before. His position with regard to things without, to other men, is from this moment altered. His intelligence is not only the passive recipient of forms from without, a mere mirror in which the increasing crowd of images confuse and threaten to obliterate each other; it becomes active and throws itself out upon phenomena with a native force, combining or analysing them—anyhow altering them, reducing them, subjecting them, imposing itself upon them. *Vivida vis animi pervicit*; it has broken the bonds which held it captive, the spiritual principle within is born; we begin to live with a life which is above nature. The point of time in our mental progress at which this change takes place [he continues] cannot be precisely marked; it is a result gradually reached, as every higher form of life is developed by insensible transition out of a lower. As physical life passes into psychical life by a succession of steps in which there is no break, so does psychical life into spiritual. This is the life [he concludes] that the higher education aspires to promote, this is the power which it cherishes and cultivates, this is the faculty to which it appeals.

I believe that this vision of the *totum scibile* as something which was, in its totality, but not of course in its detail, really knowable by an individual mind, was one that sustained Pattison through a life of emotional and practical frustration. Sustained him, but only intermittently, for the vision was of course a *mirage*, appearing on an infinitely receding horizon; and with his moments of illumination alternated moments of despair.

A year or so before he died, Pattison read the newly

published *Journal Intime* of Amiel. He was so moved by it that he addressed a letter to its editor, Edmond Scherer, which was printed by Mrs Humphry Ward in the introduction to her translation of Amiel, which came out two years after Pattison's death.

I wish to convey to you, sir [wrote Pattison to Scherer], the thanks of one at least of the public for giving the light to this precious record of a unique experience. I say unique, but I can vouch that there is in existence at least one other soul which has lived through the same struggles, mental and moral, as Amiel. In your pathetic description of the *volonté qui voudrait vouloir, mais impuissante à se fournir à elle-même des motifs,*—of the repugnance for all action—the soul petrified by the sentiment of the infinite, in all this I recognise myself...As I cannot suppose that so peculiar a psychological revelation will enjoy a wide popularity, I think it a duty to the editor to assure him that there are persons in the world whose souls respond, in the depths of their inmost nature, to the cry of anguish which makes itself heard in the pages of these remarkable confessions.

'Petrified by the sentiment of the infinite': that was his feeling in moods of depression. He put it to himself in his Diary not many months before he died: 'Reading promiscuously, without effort or aim, soon palls—and I find myself perpetually asking Why should I give myself the trouble to learn this? Why not doze through the remnant of life, as I have seen other old people do? The fact is, I cannot. I am impelled by an invisible force, to be always refilling the vessel of the Danaides.'

On his deathbed he came nearer than he had ever come before to communicating the secret of the 'invisible force' that had dominated his life. Not many hours before he died, he was led, said his widow, to speak of his creed: 'His broken utterances came forth with a passionate energy such as revealed the profound depth of his faith and conviction.' This is what he said:

To the philosopher God means the highest conceivable value, it is the thing *per se*, it is intellect. Whether it belongs to an individual or is a diffused essence...we don't know. Aristotle thought it was a portion of a diffused essence escaping—what becomes of it we don't know—of its psychical nature we are absolutely ignorant.

All the philosopher can do in life is to bear in mind that its moral value as a possession is transcendent. If ever you have realised its existence, lay hold of it, never let it go—the life of the soul will give you joy beyond all other joys; if you have ever known it let nothing carry you away from it, for if you do the world will be too strong for you. Remember that the momentary visitations of being are worth any objects of ambition—moments of realisation of self, if self it is. There is no such joy as this, hold it if you once have seen your way to it, keep it fast.

The Positivists gets no further than Bacon, no further than the idea of 'fruit', of the conquest of nature by the intelligence—apprehending its relations—all *that* is only the substratum or basis of the grand development of thought which provides not only for my seventy years of life, but for the past and present, which pervades all things.

The greater part of mankind have no mind, or circumstances have not developed it. Yet the whole of this ideal order of intellect is only a scaffolding on which is built up the grand conception of the universe as a totality governed by fixed laws. The true slavery is that of the 'doers' to the free idle philosopher who lives not to do, or enjoy, but to know.

That was the faith Pattison died in, and the faith he lived for: he believed that the attainment of a philosophical view of the universe (or of some department of the universe) was the highest aim that an individual mind could set itself; a university was an association of individuals occupied in pursuing that aim. His personal ideal was linked with and inspired his idea of a university.

Pattison, you will remember, at an early stage of his career, expressed himself scornfully about the lecture as an instrument of the higher education. He regarded it as a vehicle suitable for conveying facts, or superficial presentations of theory, to a youthful or *dilettante* audience. He was contemptuous of 'elegant epideictic orations delivered by professors (in the French "Faculties of Letters") not to the students, but to a miscellaneous audience of ladies and gentlemen who come and go during the hour, and who manifest by frequent applause their gratification at the intellectual treat they are enjoying'. Later, he came to believe that the *rôle* of the lecturer, if rightly used, could be made to serve the true purpose of education— a lecturer could help his hearers to see deeper into things, to rearrange their ideas, to improve their minds.

One who has chosen to lecture about Pattison ought not to shirk the application of that test to his own discourses. What, then, can I hope to have achieved by this series of lectures beyond, at best, mere entertainment, the serving up of a collection of facts and anecdotes and cursory, superficial judgements, which help to pass three or four hours without intolerable tedium? Have I given you anything *to take away*?

Is there, you may ask—and Pattison would himself have been the first to put the question—is there any lesson to be drawn from what I have told you about him? What effect did he and his ideas produce in his own time, what relevance have they for ours?

Well! it is difficult to measure the personal influence that strong characters exert, not only on the society in which they live, but even upon after-generations, simply by being what they are. And Pattison's strongly individual character, and his dedication of his considerable mental powers to an intellectual ideal, must have made an impression on many of his contemporaries, and may have altered, to a degree that we cannot now estimate, their attitude towards the important things in life.

Let me borrow, with only slight amendments, the words of a novelist who was his contemporary:

Certainly the determining acts of his life were not ideally beautiful. They were the result of noble impulse struggling amidst conditions in which pent feelings will often take the aspect of error and great faith the aspect of illusion...His finely touched spirit had still its fine issues, though they were not widely visible...The effect of his being on those around him was incalculably diffusive: for the growing good of the world is partly dependent on unhistoric acts; and that things are not so ill with you and me as they might have been, is half owing to the number who lived faithfully a hidden life, and rest in unvisited tombs.

You will have recognized—though I have changed the genders, for the writer had in mind not Pattison but (I suspect) his wife—the closing paragraphs of *Middlemarch*.

So, if I have introduced any of you to Pattison, or

made you better acquainted with him, if I have gained a new reader for his *Memoirs*, or aroused curiosity enough to induce any of you to follow up some of the clues I have dropped about his personal life, I may have done something to perpetuate the influence of his example. Some of you may become, as many of his contemporaries must have been, if not 'the better', at least different, for having known him.

But, you may still ask, what about his practical efforts to reform the academic systems of his day? How far were they effective? And, effective or not, have his writings about universities—the evidence he submitted to the two Commissions, his *Suggestions on Academical Organisation*, his contribution to *Essays on the Endowment of Research*—any intrinsic value? And have they any relevance to the problems of the present day? Did his contemporaries listen to what he said? Is there any reason why we should listen to it now?

Pattison, of course, was prominent in the two successive movements for university reform that occurred in the 'forties and again twenty years later. But I do not think that he positively influenced the direction taken by either movement. Reform, on each occasion, was bound to come, and there were plenty of liberals, without his assistance, to see it through. And when it did come, it did not come in the way he wanted it. In 1851 he stood out unsuccessfully, and in opposition to his fellow-reformers, against the strengthening of the professoriate and the admission of non-collegiate students; and if substantial effect was given by the Commission of 1877 to his plea that the college endowments should be transferred to the University, his hopes were not fulfilled by the reforms that actually took place.[1] He never lived to see Oxford transformed into the national institute of learning that he longed for. His controversial efforts, like his whole life, if you apply to them the test of practical and instant success, must be judged to have missed their mark. But that was largely because his ideas were in advance of his time.

If you read the literature generated by the Oxford controversies of a hundred years ago—and the volume of it is enormous—you will find that the greater part of it, while it throws a vivid light on the life and thought and atmosphere of the University at that time, is of merely 'historical' interest; but there are three writers who stand out from the rest because they do not 'date', and whose utterances are as relevant to our present-day problems as to those of their own contemporaries: Matthew Arnold, Newman and Mark Pattison.

Newman in his various discourses on the Idea of a University strips the problems of their temporal details and discusses the underlying issues *sub specie aeternitatis*: in this, no less than in the speaking persuasiveness of his style,

---

[1] 'When that volume [*Academical Organisation*, 1868] was published', he wrote in his *Memoirs* in 1883, 'its recommendations seemed so startling and paradoxical that very few dared to declare themselves in their favour. Within less than twenty years the colleges and the University have been arranged by a Commission in conformity with the spirit, if not the letter, of my proposals.' The rearrangement was in practice far from satisfying him: it realized the forebodings expressed in the passages quoted above (p. 124) from his letter to Appleton and his contribution to *Essays on the Endowment of Research*.

he reminds one irresistibly of Plato. Pattison is Aristotelian, always extremely practical, and concerned with ways and means, with facts and figures. His writings about university matters are full of budgets and statistical tables, of detailed analyses and schemes of organization; but he never loses sight of his ideal of a university, and his ideal was in no way circumscribed or determined by the then existing state of things. If he was an out-and-out radical, he was also a far-seeing one, and it is this combination of radicalism and farsightedness that keeps what he says alive today.

For example, he spends many pages in his *Suggestions* discussing in detail the redistribution of the endowments of the colleges; but before embarking on this discussion he quite coolly makes the following observation: 'No one will dispute that we are now'—he was writing in 1867–8— 'in a transitional period of society in this country—i.e. Society is not now organised for permanence. When it is so organised we may then do without endowments. The nation will then want nothing which it does not pay for out of the annual taxes.' There cannot have been many members of Oxford common rooms in the 1860s who looked forward with such certainty, and such complacent certainty, to the nationalization of higher education. For Pattison that prospect held no terrors; he would have regarded it as natural and logical that a national institution should be paid for—and, if paid for, controlled—by the nation.

What, today, are the main broad problems that trouble those concerned with the planning of higher education in this country?

First, expansion: how to provide for large numbers

seeking admission; whether any candidate who desires a university education should be denied one; if selection is necessary, by what principles it should be governed; and, more particularly, how to relate university studies to the curriculum of the schools from which those seeking matriculation are drawn.

Then, the position of the natural sciences; is it essential to the being of a university that it should accommodate the full range of them? Would a university deserve to be so called if it catered only for the natural sciences, or only for the humanities? And how are the claims of the one to be adjusted to the other's? The same problem presents itself in relation to the curriculum: should not every one who studies science at the University be taught, if only to save appearances, at least a smattering of the humanities—Homer, perhaps, in translation—and every humanist at least—well!—the second law of thermodynamics?

Then, what kind of education should a university offer? Should it attempt to provide vocational or technical training, and how far is it possible to combine such training with an education truly liberal?

There is no doubt where Pattison would have stood, in his own day, on each of the main issues I have mentioned. He was unreservedly in favour of university extension; he was an uncompromising supporter of the sciences; and he had no doubt that it was the function of a university to provide for the young not a training for a particular trade or profession, but an education scientific in a sense both broader and deeper than that attaching to the ordinary use of the word.

But, though these same questions present themselves in our day as in his, the society in relation to which they arise has so changed that the meaning of the questions themselves has altered. When you consider the problem of admissions to the University and the problem of meeting the claims of science, you see at once that the nature of these problems has been entirely transformed, if only by reason of the increase in the scale of the factors involved—the numbers, and the cost. And when you consider the nature of the education to be provided, you see that the problem has been given a new complexion by the spread of primary and secondary education. Pattison's contemporaries could afford, when they thought about university education, to disregard the great mass of the public, which was, literally, uneducated and did not, of course, even dream of coming to Oxford or Cambridge; today, that great mass has obtained the *entrée* to the universities, and it is all the more difficult to cater for because the aims that impel these thousands of students to matriculate in each year are so diverse, and because many of them have not had the thorough general education that Pattison regarded as a necessary preparation for higher studies.

'The ideal of a national university', Pattison said, 'is that it should be co-extensive with the nation.' What he meant by 'co-extensive with the nation' becomes plain when he goes on to say, 'If we can only draft in 500, say 300, students (additional) from a class whose education has hitherto terminated with the national school, or the commercial academy...it would be the beginning of a system by which the University would strike its roots freely into the subsoil of society, and draw from it new elements of life, and substance of mental and moral power.'

300 or 500! The number of 'additional students' who must be 'drafted' into the universities in the twenty years ending in 1980 is, according to Lord Robbins' Report, not 300, nor 3,000, nor 300,000, but 350,000.[1]

What kind of education can the universities provide for them? And what kind of education do they want?

What at least is plain is that not one in a hundred of them —I had almost said, one in a thousand—wants knowledge for its own sake, mental culture, help towards achieving the philosophic apprehension of a *totum scibile* that allured Pattison throughout his life, the beatific vision that he testified to on his deathbed. If they 'repair to Cambridge' their first aim is not 'to improve their minds'. Some of them, no doubt, are impelled by the desire of obtaining, if not a truly 'higher' education, at least that general education to provide which Pattison thought was the function of a superior school, not of a university. But the vast majority, it can hardly be denied, flock to the university like sheep, simply in order to be able 'to bleat B.A., B.A., B.A.!' after their names and to go on 'B-Litt'ing after they have taken their first degree—in plain language, to get the qualification for a business or profession, or for further academic employment, that is conferred by a university degree. It is in order to satisfy this need that

---

[1] 'The best available estimates', we are now told (in an authoritative article in *The Times Literary Supplement*, 19 May 1966), 'suggest far higher figures than appear in the [Robbins] Report.'

colleges of technology are to become 'up-graded' to the status of universities, so that, without any alteration of the training that they give, they may confer degrees upon their students. One could hardly have a better example of the ingenuous British habit of believing that you can alter the nature or the value of things by changing their names. Still, it is better that technical colleges should be called universities than that universities should become institutes of technology.

I think I know what Pattison would have said to such aspirants to his university: he would have said, 'We don't want *you*!'—not out of any disrespect for the student— there is no cause for shame in wishing to be qualified for your profession—but because to grant such qualifications is not the function of a university.

'It is no part of the proper business of a University', Pattison told the Social Science Congress at Liverpool in 1876, 'to be a professional school. Universities are not to fit men for some special mode of gaining a livelihood; their object is not to teach law or divinity, banking or engineering, but to cultivate the mind and form the intelligence. A University should be in possession of all science and all knowledge, but it is as science and knowledge, not as a money-bringing pursuit, that it possesses it'; and here he takes exactly the same stand as Matthew Arnold: 'The aim and office of instruction, say many people, is to make a man a good citizen, or a good Christian or a gentleman; or it is to fit him to get on in the world, or it is to enable him to do his duty in that state of life to which he is called. It is none of these', says Arnold, 'and the modern spirit more and more discerns it to be none of these. These are at best secondary and indirect aims of instruction; its prime direct aim is to enable a man *to know himself and the world.*'

I have quoted Pattison and Arnold. If their language and their outlook seem old fashioned, let me quote from another authority whose idiom is at least up to date, and whose opinions may suggest that the dangers against which they uttered their warnings are still to be reckoned with. Let me quote from an essay contributed by the Chaplain of the University of Sussex to a recently published symposium on 'Unity and Diversity in Higher Education'—a modern counterblast to *Essays on the Endowment of Research.* 'The educated society', says this writer, and he says it with apparent satisfaction, 'is the kind of society into which we are moving'; it is a society 'in which paper qualifications obtained through formal education increasingly become the chief factors in determining the function and status of most people'.

Like Arnold and Pattison, the Chaplain is concerned with the relation between a liberal and a vocational education; unlike them he is evidently anxious to persuade us that there is no difference (or 'no ultimate contradiction') between the two:

We urgently need a fresh and *more positive understanding* of the vocational element in education [he says]. A very large part of education is vocational, but people are often reluctant to admit it and do not *approach it constructively enough.* It may be one of the *great insights* brought by *the Biblical understanding of man* that there need be *no ultimate contradiction* between liberal and vocational education. Provided the job fulfils a worthwhile human need and is *seen in enough depth* and *in a wide enough context*, preparation for it helps to give *a sense of purpose* and *the discipline of life as it is* to academic study.

'A positive understanding'; 'a constructive approach'; 'seen in depth'; 'in a wide enough context'; 'a sense of purpose'; 'the great insights'—these pulpit *clichés*, and that delightful if ambiguous phrase 'the Biblical understanding of man', suggest that the writer has not thought out clearly several important distinctions between the things he has in mind: a distinction between different kinds of job; a distinction between different kinds of education; and a distinction between different kinds of value-judgement. Since such confusions are common in current discussions about higher education, it is worth while looking a little more closely into his pronouncement.

What the Chaplain is saying seems to be this: 'A large proportion of those who ask for an education today want it simply because it gives them a necessary qualification for a job. A technical education is, therefore, all they need and all that they receive. We ought not on that account to look down on them: the New Testament tells us that such people may deserve to go to Heaven just as much as people who have received the most liberal education a university can provide. Moreover', he seems to suggest, 'since the product of one kind of education is not superior to the product of the other, it is wrong to regard a liberal education itself as superior to a vocational education; indeed, the distinction between the two is fundamentally a false one; a vocational education, if it is undertaken in the right spirit, *is* a liberal education; and if it is viewed in the right spirit, it will be seen to be a liberal education.'

Given his theological premises, the Chaplain's first conclusion is a sound one: no doubt, in the eyes of God, if what we are told about Him in the New Testament is true, the most ignorant artisan may be as near to the Kingdom of Heaven as the most richly cultivated philosopher. And many people who do not share the Chaplain's religious beliefs would none the less agree with him that the moral worth of an individual is not to be measured by the depth of his culture. But this is a moral judgement, reached by applying only ethical criteria; if we take a larger view, we have to admit that, as a specimen of the flowering of the human race, a humanist of the Renaissance or an eighteenth-century *philosophe* (to take examples from the past) is superior to a cave-man or one of Attila's Huns, just as a Fellow of the Royal Society or a Justice of the Supreme Court of the United States (to take examples from the present day) must be ranked above an aborigine from New Guinea or an African savage. Moreover, although it makes sense to talk of two individuals as being equally, or in different degrees, good in a moral sense, the concept of moral equality or superiority has no application to different kinds of education; it means nothing to call one kind of education 'better' or 'worse', in this sense, than any other.[1]

But the author of the passage quoted is evidently anxious to compare the values of two kinds of education, the vocational and the liberal, and to persuade us that each

---

[1] Except in so far as it inculcates virtue or vice, or tends to strengthen or sap the moral character.

is as 'good' as the other; half aware, perhaps, of the impossibility of doing this, he suggests that there is, at bottom, no difference—or, as he puts it, 'no ultimate contradiction'—between them.

I am not sure that I understand how one kind of education could 'contradict' another; but I think I see what the writer means, and if I am right it is something like the opposite of the truth.

Vocational educations, of course, differ from each other as widely as do the vocations they are respectively designed for; but, speaking generally, one may say that the larger the technical content of an educational course, and the more strictly it is designed for a particular kind of job, the less liberal will be the education that it provides.

To appreciate why this should be so, one must pay attention to two distinctions that the writer has overlooked or dismissed as irrelevant—a distinction between different kinds of job or calling, and a distinction between different purposes for which educational courses may be designed.

Some professions or vocations can be practised or followed with perfect success by persons of little or no general culture. This is true of chess, for instance, and of pure mathematics; it is also true of many industrial occupations, especially those that consist of manual work or work that involves nothing more than the application of a technique; for many such mechanized jobs intelligence and imagination are said to be positively a handicap. Such occupations may well be called soul-destroying, and in an education designed solely to provide a training for them there is no room for any liberal element.

On the other hand, there are callings—not many, if the truth must be told—in which there is scope, or even need, for general culture, for the exercise of judgement and imagination about human activities, faculties that can be trained and fed by knowledge of the world and human nature and reflexion upon them. Such are the professions of the historian, the novelist, the teacher, the legislator and the statesman, each of whom if he has received a liberal education may do what he has to do the better for it.[1]

If a course of education is designed as a training for a vocation, the extent of the liberal element in it (if any) will depend in the first instance upon what kind of vocation it is designed for. It will also depend upon how strictly its aim is limited to training the pupil for a particular calling; if it contains a liberal element over and above what serves the purposes of that calling, the designer of the course must be presumed to have had in mind (whether he knew it or not) another educational object besides vocational training.

For there is another kind of education, distinguishable from vocational training by the aim that inspires it, and it is to this that the Chaplain must be referring, whether or not he fully appreciates what it is, when he speaks of a liberal education. It is the kind of education that Arnold and Pattison described as higher or humane education, and it is the kind of education that they supposed that a university (in so far as it is more than an institute for

[1] To that limited extent a liberal education may serve the purpose of a vocational training—a truth that may lurk in the Chaplain's statement that the two are not, in the end, mutually contradictory; but I do not know where in the Bible he can have learned it.

learning) existed to provide. Its aim is what Pattison called 'mental culture'—in Matthew Arnold's phrase, acquiring knowledge of the world and of one's self. Cultivating the mind does not, of course, mean simply sharpening the wits, any more than knowing the world means simply accumulating facts; while the object of a technical training is to produce the skilled operator, in one field or another, the object of a liberal education is to produce the perfected mind, not as an instrument for use in any field at all. In other words, while a vocational education is a training for work, a liberal education (if it is to be reckoned a training at all) is a training for leisure; it teaches, as Pattison put it, the art to live: it instructs a man how to live and move in the world and look upon it as befits a civilized being.

A hundred years ago, the function of Oxford and Cambridge was to educate a small, leisured, governing class. Whether the education they provided for that class was a truly liberal one might have been questioned—it was indeed questioned by Pattison himself, who thought that half the undergraduates came up to idle, and half of them to cram for degrees—but it was certainly not in any narrow or specific sense vocational, and it helped to teach the art of life to those who ruled the nation.

Today responsibility for governing the country is no longer the privilege of a small class, any more than is the opportunity of enjoying a university education; and the proportion of leisure hours in the life of the nation has hugely increased.

It would seem certain that, in a hundred years' time, if

democracy survives in this country, and if the pace of mechanization in industry does not slacken, preponderant leisure, like the responsibility for government, will be universal; the scope for the benefits of a liberal education will thus be infinitely extended and the need for it, if civilized values are to be preserved, intensified.

In the meantime, we are passing through a period in which, for political reasons, vocational education is being given unprecedented encouragement; we are continually being told that there is a national need for increased provision of advanced technological training, especially in the field of science and industry. A liberal education, therefore, is under attack at the very time when the need for its preservation is most urgent. The attack, of course, is not frontal; humane values are not decried, but other values are exalted at their expense or alleged to be indistinguishable from them. The process is aided in the field of education by appeals made to moral concepts, such as social justice, without any adequate attempt on the part of those who make them to define the things they are talking about or to estimate their comparative values. A fellow of an Oxford College, writing on 'Expansion and Traditional Values' in the same symposium as the Sussex chaplain, declares, in the name of 'educational justice', that Lord Robbins's Committee 'showed too much concern for "maintaining standards"'; 'standards', she says, 'must be shaped to the people rather than the people to the standards', and 'we must finally abandon our hurtful and misleading notion that "vocational" and "non-vocational" form the inferior and superior tiers of higher education'. 'The vocational shape to an academic purpose', she continues (exactly what she means by 'shape' is not quite clear), 'has always been a legitimate and worthy one, for there is a fundamental human value in setting out to acquire expertise of a high order for use in human society.' Like the chaplain, this writer is really echoing George Herbert: *Who sweeps a room, as for thy laws*—or for the betterment of human society—*Makes that, and the action, fine*. No doubt; but is it a proper function of a university in this country—as it is assumed to be in some universities in the United States—to teach household management? The planning of courses of study at Colleges of Advanced Technology, so as to interweave a genuinely liberal strand with the vocational education that they offer, is a matter of the greatest importance and offers problems of the greatest difficulty. One is not much reassured about the way these problems are being tackled when one is told that 'Over the past few years technical colleges of various types and colleges of education have been hard at work shaping courses which can genuinely be claimed as higher education'. The pathetic words 'can genuinely be claimed as higher education' suggest that those making the claim have no clear and adequate conception of a liberal education as I have described it, and the prophecy that 'a fruitful marriage of technology and education...might bear issue in a new type of vocational and humane university' sounds less like an enlightened forecast than a muddled, if pious, profession of faith. Could such a union take place without debasing 'traditional values'? The same writer gives us her answer: 'Whether the process be termed "adaptation" or "dilution", traditional values must undergo modification to meet the needs of expansion.'

I quote these passages not in mockery of those who wrote them, still less in disparagement of the students to whom in effect they refer, but in order to point a contrast with the passages I quoted earlier from Pattison himself. That contrast ought to make us think. The problems involved by the necessity of expansion and of specialization; how to relate the humanities and the physical sciences as disciplines for the training of the growing mind; how to ensure that somehow those who require a prolonged technological training do not emerge from it without any appreciation of issues and values that lie outside the field of their immediate concern—these are real and difficult and important problems. But they will not be solved by supposing that a vocational training and a liberal education are interchangeable, or by assuming that, because a liberal education has something to contribute to training for some vocations (it may make a man a better magistrate, for instance, or a better civil servant), therefore any kind of vocational training (if it is 'approached constructively', or 'seen in enough depth') is itself a liberal education. The two things are different; nothing is gained, and much of the best that a university has to offer may be irreparably lost, by pretending that the difference between them does not exist or that, if it does exist, it does not matter.